English Code 5

Workbook

Contents

OUR WORLD

INTRO:

Here we stand: children of every age,
This is our world and the world's our stage.
We can laugh, we can cry – we can float, we can fly,
We can dance, we can sing – we can do almost anything
in OUR world ... our *beautiful* world.

VERSE 1:

Some of us are small; some of us are tall,
Some of us are shy; some say hi to everybody,
Some of us like numbers; some of us love words,
Some of us watch football, and some of us watch the birds!

(CHORUS)

This is our world ... we're different but the same.
We live and learn together – we get to know each other ...
in OUR world ... our *beautiful* world.

VERSE 2:

Some of us like music; some of us like cars,
Some of us draw pictures, looking at the stars,
Some of us are scientists, trying to find the code,
All of us can help a friend and give a hand to hold.

This is our world – there's room for everyone.
We learn to live together, and we have a lot of fun ...
In **our** world ... in **our** world ... in our beautiful world!

3

Progress chart

Unit 8

Unit 7

Unit 6

Unit 5

Unit 4

Unit 3

Unit 2

Unit 1

Creativity

Collaboration

Critical Thinking

Coding

Communication

Welcome!

 How can I talk about my neighborhood?

1 **Look at Student's Book page 5. Create your own *Neighbor of the Month* factfile.**

2 **Read and complete. Then listen and check.**

boxes   hobbies   lives   name   world

People in my neighborhood have interesting **1** _____ . Our neighbor, Mrs. Drake, collects plates. She brings them from all over the **2** _____ . Do you have a neighbor with interesting hobbies?

Another neighbor, Mr. Green, is very friendly and helps with things like carrying heavy **3** _____ . Do you have friendly neighbors?

My best friend **4** _____ at number 24. Her **5** _____ is Abby. I go to her house on the weekends to play board games. Do you have a friend who lives near you?

3 **Complete the sequences.**

CODE CRACKER

a	2	____	6	8	____	____	14
b	3	5	____	____	11	13	____
c	72	82	92	____	112	____	
d	99	____	95	____	91	____	

4 **Play *Word Categories – Stop!***

A first name:

Fred

_____

A last name:

Fernandez

_____

A hobby:

fishing

_____

Furniture in a house:

fridge

_____

A place:

farm

_____

Our neighborhood

VOCABULARY

1 Read the definitions and write the words.

1 a fun name that people call you   _____

2 the name your parents gave you   _____

3 the name you share with other family members   _____

4 the people who live near you   _____

2 Read about where Jenny lives. Then complete the chart.

I live in an apartment building with a great view. I can see mountains and trees from my window. But our apartment is small and noisy. I don't have my own room and can't get away from my sisters.

One good thing about our building is the neighbors are friendly. If we need something, we can ask for help.

There is a small supermarket and a bus stop on our street. Mom says it is convenient for going downtown.

Our neighborhood is nice, but there aren't many parks. It's a little bit boring for children.

Good things	Bad things
It has a great view.	It's small and noisy.

3 Complete the chart about where you live.

Things you like	Things you don't like
_____	_____
_____	_____
_____	_____
_____	_____
_____	_____

4 Complete the sentences.

movers   housewarming party
blended family   residence

1 The place where I live is my

_____.

2 I have a dad, a stepmom, a stepbrother, and two half-sisters. We are a

_____.

3 Would you like to come over to our house? There will be music and food. We are having a _____.

4 People who pack your things and take them to your new house are called

_____.

Language lab 1

GRAMMAR: -WHERE, -ONE, -THING

1 Read and complete.

> everyone   everywhere   everything   somewhere   anywhere

My Well-Traveled Neighbor

My neighbor Tony has been almost **1** _____ in the world! He loves to talk about his travels, and tells **2** _____ about his adventures. Before Tony goes **3** _____ new, he reads all about the place on the internet. He likes to know **4** _____ about the place before he goes. Where would you go if you could go **5** _____ ?

2 Now listen and check your answers.

3 Unscramble the words and complete the sentences.

> oaynne   wynreahe   ythaning   onnthig

1   Is there _____ good to eat in your fridge?

2   Is there _____ good to eat in your town?

3   Do you know _____ who rides a motorcycle to school?

4   What day of the week do you like to relax and do _____ ?

4 In pairs, ask and answer the questions in 3.

5 Read and solve the math problem.

MATH ZONE

There are 36 people on my street. One third are women, one third are men, and one third are children. Of the children, half are girls. How many boys live on our block?

_____

I can use general words, e.g., everywhere, everyone, everything.

Story lab

I will read a story about getting to know neighbors.

1 💡 **Read, look at the pictures, and match.**

1 Tom looked out of the window and saw Hoops and Rebecca waving at him. He did know someone at the street party!

2 "Wait!" said Hoops. "My first name is Peter, but my nickname is Hoops. People usually call me Hoops because I love basketball."

Tom gave the letter to Hoops.

3 First, Tom tried apartment 302. A girl opened the door.

Her name wasn't Peter Adams, it was Rebecca Williams.

2 💬 **Write the answers. Then ask and answer in pairs.**

1 Did you live in the same house last year or have you moved recently?

_____

2 Is there anyone new on your block or in your apartment building?

_____

3 Are you or is anyone else new at school this year?

_____

4 How can you be kind to a new person at school?

_____

5 Do you like meeting new people?

_____

3 ☎ 004 **Listen and write.**

A: What's your name?

B: I'm **1** _____ . How about you?

A: I'm **2** _____ . What's your last name, Nick?

B: My surname is **3** _____ . And yours?

A: My last name is **4** _____ . Nice to meet you **5** _____ !

B: Nice to meet you **6** _____ !

4 💬 **Practice the conversation in 3 with a partner. Use your names.**

5 **What do you do when you meet someone new? Check ☑ .**

In my country, we smile at each other. ☐

In my country, we bow. ☐

In my country, we shake hands. ☐

1 Time for school

How do we design our ideal school?

1 Read and sort.

open air   books   lesson   model   flower   vegetable   gardening   trees   schoolyard   learn

Classroom	Greenhouse	Outside

2 Solve the math problems to find the secret message. Use the code.

CODE CRACKER

1	2	3	4	5	6	7	8	9	10	11	12	13	14	15	16
a	e	i	o	u	b	c	f	j	m	n	r	s	t	v	l

___ ___ ___ ___ ___ ___ ___ ___ ___ ___ ___ ___

$12÷4$ $4×4$ $10−6$ $9+6$ $10÷5$ $9+4$ $11−4$ $12÷4$ $14÷7$ $6+5$ $4+3$ $14−12$

3 Read and complete. Then listen and check your answers.

make   take care of   grow   read   water

In gardening class, we **1** _____ books about how to **2** _____ flowers and plants and **3** _____ vegetables. Then we go outside and do some gardening! When it's hot, we **4** _____ the flowers and vegetables more frequently using a new watering system. I'm going to **5** _____ a model of the watering system and give a presentation about how it works.

4 What outdoor activities do you do at school? Ask and answer.

I plant things.   I do experiments.   I tidy up.

School life

VOCABULARY

I will learn words to describe education and learning.

1 Circle the odd one out.

1   lunch / experiment / equipment

2   backpack / pajamas / lunch box

3   make a model / take a test / make your bed

4   outside / principal / classmate

5   inside / soccer field / playground

2 (006) Listen, read, and circle T (True) or F (False).

1   Harry's talking about his English class.   T / F

2   He's making a model volcano.   T / F

3   Sally likes math.   T / F

4   She has a test on addition and subtraction.   T / F

5   In Helen's favorite class, they only do
    painting.   T / F

3 Complete the sentences.

model   practice   equipment   uniform   outside

1   If you want to be good at playing the piano, you
    need to _____ every day.

2   I love going _____ at recess.

3   When you design things it's a good idea to draw
    pictures or make a _____ .

4   Some children wear a _____
    at school.

5   You usually need special _____
    when you do a science experiment.

4 (007) Listen and label the pictures.

goggles   dictionary
exam   certificate

_____   _____

_____   _____

5 Ph Say the tongue twisters as quickly as you can.

a   I think I'll drink a pink drink on Thursday.

b   Some silly swinging monkeys are singing songs.

I can use words to describe education and learning.

Language lab

GRAMMAR: EXPRESSING RULES WITH *MUST*

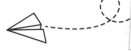

I will express rules using **must** and **mustn't**.

1 Read and circle the correct words.

1 You (must) / mustn't touch any of the objects in the museum.
2 You (must) / mustn't bring backpacks into the museum.
3 The museum closes at 6. You (must) / mustn't leave at 5:45.
4 No animals allowed. You must / (mustn't) come into the museum with pets.
5 No photos allowed. You must / (mustn't) take photos.

2 Complete the rules with must or mustn't. Then write G (Gym), L (Library), or S (Science lab).

  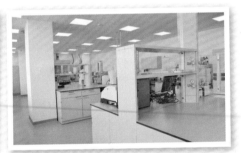

1 You _____ wear sports clothes to play volleyball. ____
2 You _____ wash and put away equipment after you do an experiment. ____
3 You _____ eat or drink on the basketball court. ____
4 You _____ take your books back before the return date. ____
5 You _____ remove the magazines from the reading area. ____
6 You _____ listen to the safety instructions when you do an experiment. ____

3 Make a poster with class rules using must/mustn't.

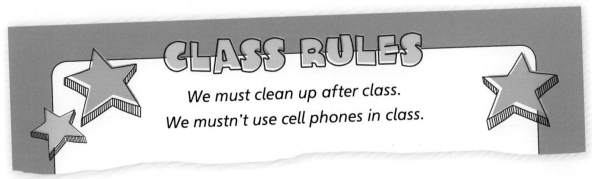

CLASS RULES

We must clean up after class.
We mustn't use cell phones in class.

4 008 **Listen and number. Write a rule for each photo.**

stop / red light   clean up / after pets   drop / litter

1 _____

2 _____

3 _____

5 **Read the article and write the rules below.**

WORLD'S **BIGGEST** MAZE

Do you know where the world's largest maze is located? It's in China and it's called the *Dream Maze*. There are many different paths in the *Dream Maze*. The walls of the paths are tall hedges. There are resting places inside the maze. There's a lot of walking to do inside the maze and people can get tired. It's a good idea to wear the right clothes and strong shoes because the paths have rocks and stones. There's no water inside the maze, so it's important to bring a bottle of water. Most importantly, don't lose your family and friends in the maze, especially your children. The maze opens at 10 a.m. and closes at 5 p.m. Don't leave anyone inside the maze!

1 (wear walking shoes) _____

2 (bring water) _____

3 (watch your children) _____

4 (leave at 5 p.m.) _____

5 (forget anyone) _____

I can express rules using must and mustn't .

Story lab

READING

I will read a story about robots in a school.

THE ROBOT HELPERS

1 **Read the beginning and the end of *The Robot Helpers* and complete the sentences.**

When I was eleven, our school principal was a woman called Mrs. Miller. She was crazy about computers and robots. One morning, she said, "I have a surprise for you. Meet our amazing new robots. They're here to help us!"

The robots couldn't open the doors, so they couldn't go outside. They moved more and more slowly, and finally, they stopped. Mrs. Miller took out their batteries and we were all happy!

…

"Thanks, kids," said Mrs. Miller. "I'm not keen on robots now!"

1   Mrs. Miller was the _____ of the school.

2   She liked _____ in the beginning.

3   In the end Mrs. Miller took out the robots' _____ .

4   She _____ keen on robots in the end.

2 **Circle the things in the story.**

computers	cats	robots	surprise	breakfast
homework	equipment	the world	the soccer field	floor
bedroom	screen	message	solar panels	power
keys	doors	outside	batteries	

3 Number the sentences in order.

a *First*, Mrs. Miller brought robots to school to help the students. _____

b *Suddenly*, the robots wanted to take over the world, destroy the classrooms, and make more robots. _____

c *Then* the students saw the low battery and locked the doors so the robots couldn't recharge their batteries in the sunlight. _____

d *Then* the robots helped the children with their work and carried equipment. _____

e *Finally*, the robots stopped, Mrs. Miller took out the batteries, and everyone was happy. _____

4 Write an alternative ending to *The Robot Helpers*.

_____

_____

5 Your principal has some robots for you. Write a set of rules for your classroom robots.

_____

_____

_____

6 Write your opinion of the story.

Key	My opinion
1 = very bad 5 = very good	My favorite character is _____ . My favorite part is _____ . I think the story is interesting / funny / scary / silly . I liked / didn't like the story because _____ _____ . I think it's _____ story. I _____ and _____ .

① ② ③ ④ ⑤

I can   read a story about robots in a school.

Experiment lab

I will find out which surfaces reflect or absorb light.

1 Read and complete.

> artificial light   Electric lights   flashlight   natural light   rays   reflects   Solar

Light Quiz The sun is important because it gives us natural light. Natural light from the sun _____ off the moon. That reflection is what we see in the night sky. The moon does not produce light. The sun's _____ travel through space to warm our planet. Solar power production takes the sun's rays and turns them into electricity. _____ panels absorb heat from the sun to capture its energy and turn it into electricity. The sun is the only source of _____ .

Light that is not natural is called _____ . An example of artificial light is a _____ . It gets its energy from a battery, not the sun. _____ are another example of artificial light. We use them to light our homes, offices, and streets.

2 Match to make sentences.

1	Candles are	a	natural light.
2	Rays from the sun	b	absorb light and turn it into energy.
3	Solar panels	c	shine down and warm our planet.
4	The sun gives us	d	a form of artificial light.
5	The moon	e	reflects the sun's light.

3 Read and solve the math problem.

MATH ZONE

There has been a power cut. All the houses on Ana's street need light. Each house needs one candle per room.

House 1: six rooms   House 4: eight rooms

House 2: five rooms   House 5: nine rooms

House 3: seven rooms

How many candles should Ana buy to light the street?

_____

EXPERIMENT TIME

Report

1 Look and label the pictures.

> aluminum foil   black paper   desk   sweater   light-colored paper   wooden door

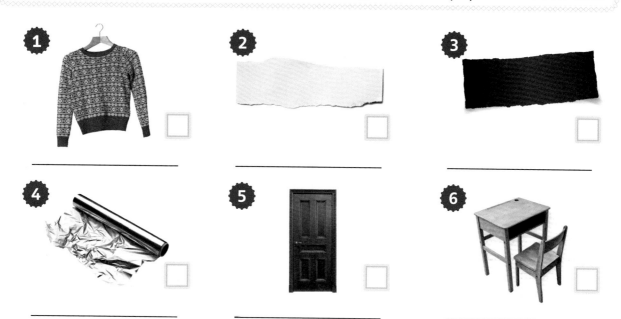

2 Look at **1** again. Check ☑ the surfaces that reflected light well in your experiment.

3 Think about <u>your</u> experiment. Complete the chart.

Materials that absorbed light	Materials that reflected light

4 Write your report.

Reflect or absorb?

White paper: White paper reflects light.

Black paper: Black paper _____ light.

Aluminum foil: Aluminum foil _____ light.

_____ : _____ reflects light.

_____ : _____ absorbs light.

_____ : _____ _____ light.

I know which surfaces reflect or absorb light.

A friend in India

COMMUNICATION

I will talk about rules using **have to** and **don't have to**.

1 🎧 009 **Listen to an interview with Karen and check ✓ the information about her.**

1 ☐ a Karen plays the piano.   ☐ b Karen plays the drums.

2 ☐ a She has to practice once a week.   ☐ b She has to practice every day.

3 ☐ a She has to take exams.   ☐ b She doesn't have to take exams.

4 ☐ a She has to wear special clothes.   ☐ b She doesn't have to wear special clothes.

5 ☐ a She has to use a special chair.   ☐ b She has to use a song book.

2 💬 **Complete the questions. Then choose a role and ask and answer.**

Interviewer: What sports or activities **1** _____ you do?

Interviewer: Do you **2** _____ practice every day?

Interviewer: Do you have to take **3** _____ or tests?

Interviewer: Do you have to **4** _____ a uniform or special clothes?

Interviewer: **5** _____ _____ have to use special equipment?

EMILY

Sport: volleyball
Practice: on Monday and Wednesday
Exams or tests: no
Uniform: yes, team uniform
Special equipment: volleyball, volleyball net

TERESA

Activity: go to art class
Attend: once a week
Practice: yes, draw in a sketchbook everyday
Exams or tests: enter an exhibition once a year
Uniform: a smock
Special equipment: paint brushes, pencils, sketchbook

3 **Complete for you. Write notes.**

Name: _____   Exams or tests: _____

Activity or sport: _____   Uniform: _____

Practice: _____   Special equipment: _____

4 💬 **Ask and answer. Use the questions in 2 and the information in 3.**

I can talk about rules using have to and don't have to .

Writing lab

INSTRUCTIONS FOR A GAME

> *I will write instructions for a game.*

1 Circle the words you know. Use a dictionary to find the meaning of the words you don't know.

play   throw   catch   hit   pick up   roll   count   take turns   win   score   try

2 Read the instructions and answer the questions.

HOW TO PLAY   WASTEPAPER BASKETBALL

EQUIPMENT: one paper ball, one clean wastepaper basket

OBJECTIVE: Play in two teams. You must score more points than the other team.

HOW TO PLAY

- Each team has to take turns. You must stand three meters away from the basket. You have to throw the ball into the wastepaper basket to score a point for your team.
- You must pick up the ball after your turn and give it to a person on the opposite team.
- You have to count points after everyone has a turn and keep score.
- You have to play three rounds. Count the score at the end of three rounds. The winning team is the one with the most points.

1   What equipment do you need for wastepaper basketball? _____

2   What's the objective of the game? _____

3   Do you have to take turns? _____

4   Do you have to pick up the ball? _____

3 Read and solve the math problems.

MATH ZONE

I score 3 points, Mark scores 5 points, Sarah scores 3 points. How many points do we score in total?

I score 5 points. My team scores a total of 25 points. What percentage of my team's points do I score?

4 Write your own variation of *Wastepaper Basketball* in your notebook.

I can write instructions for a game.

Design your ideal school

Project report

1 Complete for your ideal school.

Type of school			Vacations and homework
☐ inside	☐ outside	☐ teachers	☐ ten weeks of vacation
☐ principal	☐ robots	☐ art	☐ 15 weeks of vacation
☐ sports	☐ math	☐ activities	☐ some homework
☐ solar panels	☐ experiments	☐ equipment	☐ a lot of homework
☐ big	☐ small	☐ garden	

2 Complete your project report.

My School

Location:	Equipment:
Buildings:	Homework:
Design:	Vacation:
No. of teachers:	Rules:
Subjects:	Extra features:

3 Present your report to your class.

I can design my ideal school.

1 Look at the rules. Write sentences with have to, don't have to, must, or mustn't.

help others ✓ — We have to help others.

keep our classroom neat ✓ ✓ — We must keep our classroom neat.

wear uniform ✗ — We don't have to wear school uniform.

be late ✗ ✗ — We mustn't arrive late.

1 study for tests ✓ _____

2 play sports at school ✗ _____

3 use cell phones at school ✗ ✗ _____

4 listen to the teacher ✓ ✓ _____

2 Read and circle the correct words.

1 **Q:** Do / Does she have to practice every day?

   A: Yes, she have to / has to practice every day.

2 **Q:** Do / Does he have to take tests?

   A: No, he don't / doesn't have to take tests.

3 **Q:** Do / Does I have to wear a uniform?

   A: No, you do / don't have to wear a uniform.

4 **Q:** Does she have to / has to study music?

   A: Yes, she have to / has to study music.

3 Ask and answer.

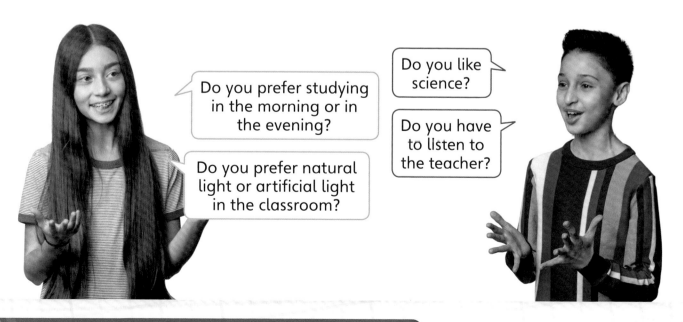

Do you prefer studying in the morning or in the evening?

Do you prefer natural light or artificial light in the classroom?

Do you like science?

Do you have to listen to the teacher?

Now go to your Progress Chart on page 4.

2 Landscapes of China

How can I make a story plate?

1 Look and write a–d. Then read and match.

1 A place with lots of trees together.

2 Land with water all around it.

3 A high area of land, sometimes with snow on top.

4 A large area of water, with land all around it.

☐ lake
☐ forest
☐ mountain
☐ island

2 Write the code. Then use it to write the sentence.

CODE CRACKER

1	2	3	4	5																		
a	b	c																				

I was walking by the lake when ...

9   19 / 1 / 23   1   4 / 18 / 1 / 7 / 15 / 14   9 / 14   20 / 8 / 5   23 / 1 / 20 / 5 / 18

_____

3 Complete the information about China with words from 1.

1 Two thirds of China is covered in _____ .

2 Qinghai is a very large salt _____ in China.

3 There are over 250 _____ in the South China Sea.

4 There's a large bamboo _____ very near Beijing.

4 Listen and check the answers to 3.

Beautiful landscapes

VOCABULARY

I will learn words to describe landscapes.

1 Complete the sentences.

jungle   desert   volcano
waterfall   lake

1 The _____ flowed from the top of the cliff down into the lake.

2 The _____ is active and lots of tourists visit every year.

3 There is very little rain in the _____ and many snakes and scorpions live there.

4 Lots of monkeys and birds live up high in the trees in the _____ .

2 🎧 011 Listen and circle T (True) or F (False).

1 Nobody ever goes to the island.   T / F
2 The island is a desert.   T / F
3 There are a lot of trees on the island. T / F
4 People hang-glide from the volcano.   T / F
5 There's a waterfall on the coast.   T / F
6 The waterfall is a popular picnic spot.   T / F

3 Correct the false statements in 2.

_____

_____

_____

_____

_____

4 🎧 012 Listen and label the pictures.

earthquake   valley   jetty   cactus

_____   _____

5 Ph 🎧 013 Read, listen, and chant. Then say the words that rhyme in pairs.

Come to the island.
And listen to the band,
Hand in hand on the sand.
Stand on the sand
And clap your hands.
Show the band that you're a fan.

I can use words to describe landscapes.

Language lab

GRAMMAR: QUESTIONS ABOUT THE PAST

I will ask questions about the past.

1 Read and circle the correct question word.

1 **What** / Where did you go?

2 How / **Who** did you see there?

3 **How** / Who did you travel?

4 **What** / When did you come home?

2 Complete with the correct question word.

1 A: _____ did you go to the museum?   B: I went yesterday.

2 A: _____ did you go with?   B: I went with my parents.

3 A: _____ told you about the museum?   B: Some friends told us about it.

4 A: _____ did you see there?   B: We saw an exhibit on Ancient China.

5 A: _____ did you have lunch?   B: We had lunch in the cafeteria.

3 Read and circle the correct words.

1 Who **lent** / did lend you that book?

2 What **happened** / did happen when the volcano erupted?

3 Who **did you go** / you went to the coast with?

4 Who buy / **bought** you that candy bar?

5 What **did you buy** / bought in the gift shop?

4 Read the story.

A Birthday Picnic

On the weekend, Shelly invited her friends to a picnic for her birthday. The picnic was in the local forest. Everyone played and had fun. They ran under the waterfall for a while.

Shelly's mom put the picnic food out on a blanket. There was chicken and salad. There was a big birthday cake as well. Then she called everyone to come and eat.

"Where's the salad?" shouted Shelly. Then the children saw the rabbits under the trees. They had the salad. They were very happy. They loved salad for lunch.

"Hurry up and eat the chicken!" said Shelly's mom.

"Mom!" shouted Shelly. "Rover's looking at my birthday cake!" The children looked at Rover. They all loved Shelly's dog, but he was famous for stealing cake.

"Let's sing Happy Birthday quickly!" said Shelly's mom. They all laughed.

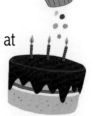

5 Write questions about the story.

1 What / they / do / last weekend?

_____

2 Why / they / go / to the forest?

_____

3 Who / put / food on the blanket?

_____

4 What / they / have?

_____

5 What / happen / to the salad?

_____

6 Who / want / eat / cake?

_____

7 Why / sing / Happy Birthday / quickly?

_____

6 In pairs, ask and answer the questions in 5.

7 Listen and answer the questions.

1 Where did Danny go? He went to _____ .

2 Who did he go with? He went with _____ .

3 What happened? A bird _____ .

8 Answer the questions for you.

1 Did you go to a museum last year?

_____

2 Who did you go with?

_____

3 What did you see?

_____

I can ask and answer questions about the past.

25

Story lab

Blue Willow

I will read a story set in ancient China.

1 Complete the information about the people in the story.

Names of characters	What do we know about them?
Lian	main character, young, and kind

2 Read and circle T (True) or F (False).

1 The story is set in China.   T / F
2 Lian was a very happy young girl.   T / F
3 She wanted to climb the mountains and see the ocean.   T / F
4 Lian's father said she could go away.   T / F
5 Chang told Lian about the green fields and beautiful birds.   T / F
6 Lian's father wanted Lian to marry Chang.   T / F

3 Answer the questions.

1 Who did Lian's father want her to marry?

_____

2 Why did Lian not like her father's suggestion?

_____

3 Who ran away with Lian?

_____

4 Where did they go?

_____

5 Why couldn't he take his daughter home?

_____

Show empathy.

4 Read and check ☑.

Lucky Chang! I'm happy for him.

Poor Chang! I'm sad for him.

1 Chang walked in the beautiful fields.
Lucky him! ☐   Poor him! ☐

2 Lian's father said she must marry Wang the farmer.
Lucky her! ☐   Poor her! ☐

3 Lian and Chang became birds.
Lucky them! ☐   Poor them! ☐

5 When you are sad, what does your body language look like? Can you identify when someone else is sad? What can you say to them?

6 Look at the picture. Check ☑ the part of the story you think it depicts. Discuss why with a partner.

1 Lian asked her father if she could go to the mountains.   ☐

2 Lian's father wanted his daughter to marry his old friend Wang.   ☐

3 Lian's father saw his daughter in the cave.   ☐

7 Write your opinion of the story.

Key	My opinion
1 = very bad	My favorite character is _____ .
5 = very good	My favorite part is _____ .

I think the story is interesting / funny / scary / silly .

I liked / didn't like the story because _____

_____ .

I think it's _____ story. I _____ and

_____ .

①   ②   ③   ④   ⑤

I can read a story set in ancient China.

Experiment lab

I will find out about the water cycle.

1 Look and write.

h_____

m_____

r_____

r_____

s_____

o_____

2 Match to make sentences.

1	Water vapor rises from	**a** into drops of liquid.
2	Water vapor condenses	**b** repeats itself.
3	Drops of liquid water	**c** from the clouds.
4	Rain, snow, or hail falls	**d** form into clouds or mist.
5	Finally the rain, snow, or hail	**e** rivers, lakes, and oceans.
6	The whole cycle	**f** returns to the lakes, rivers, and oceans.

3 Read and complete.

cools   cycle   hail   vapor   clouds

The water **1** _____ describes how water turns into water **2** _____ and
rises from lakes, rivers, and oceans. The sun heats the water and that forms the water
vapor. When the air **3** _____ , the vapor turns into drops of water and forms
4 _____ . When the clouds are big and heavy, the liquid water falls as rain,
snow, or **5** _____ .

4 Describe what happened in your rain cloud experiment.

I added two
drops and …

Then I added more
drops and …

I added more
drops and …

The stage of the rain
cycle I saw was …

5 Think about your rain cloud experiment and complete the chart.

What I already knew about rain before the experiment	What I learned about rain during the experiment	What I still want to know about rain
I already knew that …	I learned that	I still want to know …

6 Answer the questions.

1   What will the weather be like in your area tomorrow?

_____

2   Does it rain much where you live?

_____

3   Are there any mountains in your area?

_____

4   Are there any rivers?

_____

5   Do you live near a lake?

_____

I know about the water cycle.

China past and present

COMMUNICATION

I will ask questions about what life was like in the past.

1 💡 **What do people in China often have for breakfast? Check ☑.**

rice ☐   noodles ☐   toast ☐   eggs ☐   beef ☐   dumplings ☐   fruit ☐

pancakes ☐   vegetables ☐   milk ☐   soy milk ☐   orange juice ☐

2 **Read and check your answers in 1.**

The Chinese invented chopsticks 4,000 years ago in Henan Province. They made the first chopsticks out of twigs. They used them for stirring food in the cooking pot. Later the Chinese began to use chopsticks to eat their food at the table. There were knives in China before chopsticks, but Confucius, the famous Chinese philosopher, was a vegetarian. He didn't want to use knives at the table.

Did you know that Chinese people use chopsticks to eat breakfast, too? What do the Chinese eat for breakfast nowadays with their chopsticks? Most people have fried rice, fried noodles, beef, dumplings, pancakes, or vegetables. They drink milk, soy milk, or orange juice.

3 **Read the article again and answer the questions.**

1   Who invented chopsticks?

_____

_____

2   When did they invent them?

_____

_____

3   What did they first use them for?

_____

_____

4   Which philosopher said you shouldn't use knives at the table?

_____

_____

4 **Solve the math problems.** **MATH ZONE**

1   Confucius was born in 551 BCE and died in 479 BCE. How long did he live?

_____

2   The Ming Dynasty started in 1368 and ended in 1644. How long did it last?

_____

3   Matt bought four Chinese plates: a small plate for ¥120, two matching plates for ¥275 each, and a large plate for ¥525. He also bought a small vase for ¥150. How much did Matt spend in all?

_____

 **I can**   ask questions about what life was like in the past.

Writing lab

SHAPE POEMS

I will write a shape poem.

1 Complete the shape poem.

> tall   tree   drops   forest   waterfall

The
_____ in
the _____
is big, green, and _____ .
It drips excitedly with _____
from a great _____ .
Sp
la
sh!

2 **Read the poem again and draw a picture to illustrate it.**

3 **Create a shape poem called *The Lake*. You can use any of the words from the box to help you.**

> big   blue   water   streams   river   rocks
> scary   dangerous   moving   splash

The Lake

4 Check ☑ the things you find in your poem. Write the words.

color   ☐   _____

size   ☐   _____

feelings   ☐   _____

sound   ☐   _____

action   ☐   _____

5 **Read your poem to the class. Listen to the other poems.**

I can write a shape poem.

Make a story plate

1 Complete the chart for your story plate.

Who was your story about?		Where was your story set?		
☐ main character ☐ boy		☐ lake	☐ mountain	☐ island
☐ girl ☐ animal		☐ cave	☐ stream	☐ forest
other characters _____		☐ city	☐ town	☐ village
What was the problem?		**What happened?**	**What parts did you paint?**	
☐ parents ☐ friends		☐ beginning	☐ characters	☐ setting
☐ brothers ☐ sick		☐ action	☐ action	☐ beginning
☐ sisters ☐ rich		☐ ending	☐ ending	
☐ lonely ☐ poor				

2 Complete your project report.

Who was your story about?

My story was about ...

Where was your story set?

It was set ...

What was the problem?

The problem was ...

What happened?

The main character ...

What parts did you paint?

I painted ...

3 Share your report with a partner. Ask questions.

I can make a story plate.

1 Complete the summary with vocabulary from the unit.

My story was about pirates. It was set on Black Mountain Island, a small **1** i_____ with three **2** v_____ that erupted every year. Around the island, there was a rocky **3** c_____ with high cliffs and stony beaches. Pirates stood on the cliffs and looked for passing ships. Much of the island was covered in **4** f_____ . It was dark and full of spiders and mosquitoes. Pirates used the island to hide their treasure in a dark **5** c_____ behind a high **6** w_____ .

2 [015] Listen and check your answers in 1.

3 Answer the questions about 1.

1 What was the story about?

_____

2 Where was it set?

_____

3 Which animals lived on the island?

_____

4 What did the pirates use the island for?

_____

5 Where did the pirates hide their treasure?

_____

4 Complete the text with the correct form of the words. Then write the questions.

use   have   eat   go   learn   see

I'm Holly. Last week I _____ on a school trip with my friends. We went to a museum in town and saw an exhibit on China. We _____ some interesting information about Chinese history and _____ some beautiful painted plates and vases. We _____ lunch in the café and _____ chopsticks to eat our rice! Then, at 5 o'clock we got the bus home. I _____ a great day!

1 _____

_____

We went to a museum in town.

2 _____

_____

We took the bus to the museum.

3 _____

_____

We had lunch in a café.

4 _____

_____

We went home at five o'clock.

Now go to your Progress Chart on page 4.

1 Checkpoint

1 🎧 016 **Listen and follow Ellie's path.**

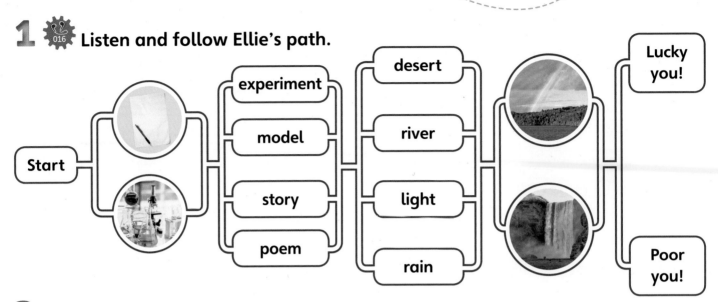

Start — experiment / model / story / poem — desert / river / light / rain — Lucky you! / Poor you!

2 **Listen to 1 again and answer the questions.**

1 What kind of competition did Ellie win?

_____

2 What did she have to do for the competition?

_____

3 What kind of experiment did she do?

_____

4 What did she win?

_____

3 **Read Kiara's email and draw her path in 1.**

Hi Pamela!

Guess what? I entered the Crowford Elementary Spring Writing Competition, and I wrote a shape poem. I had to create a poem then write it in a shape. I had to use describing and feeling words. It was difficult but I think I wrote a good poem. It was about a river that passes through many different landscapes like hills, forests, caves, and jungles as it travels thousands of kilometers from the mountains to the beach.

The prize was a vacation at a lake. And guess what again? I won! Lucky me!!

Love,

Kiara

4 Put the words in order and write questions.

1 Which / you / win / competition / did / ?

_____

2 did / you / What / to / do / ? / have

_____

3 kind of / What / ? / did / you / story / have / to write

_____

4 did / you / model / have / to make / ? / What / kind of

_____

5 What / experiment / did / kind of / to do / ? / you / have

_____

6 ? / poem / did / What / kind of / you / have to / write

_____

7 did / you / What / win / ?

_____

5 Ask and answer. Use the questions in 4 and the flowchart in 1.

Which competition did you win?

I won the science competition.

6 Write a paragraph about one of the topics.

- a competition you won
- a competition you entered
- a poem you wrote
- a story you wrote
- a science experiment you did

_____

_____

_____

_____

_____

The Outback

1 **Read about the Outback again on page 40 of your Student's Book. Circle T (True) or F (False).**

1	The Australian Outback is on the coast.	T / F
2	There are ten deserts in the Australian Outback.	T / F
3	There isn't much water in the Australian Outback.	T / F
4	Most Australians live in the Outback.	T / F
5	Most of the people that live in the Outback are farmers.	T / F
6	Some Australian farms are bigger than states in the United States.	T / F

2 **Look at the photos and read the article. Circle the best title.**

   a   Jungle Medicine
   b   Flying Doctors
   c   Nurses in the Sky

What do you do when you are sick? You probably go to see your local doctor. And if you are very sick, you go to the hospital for a few days. But it's completely different if you live in the Australian Outback. There are no doctors there, and no hospitals, either. So, what do people do when they are sick? They call the Flying Doctor Service!

The Flying Doctor Service takes care of the health of people living in the Outback. Doctors fly in planes long distances to see patients on farms. They bring nurses and medicines with them. It's an excellent service. Flying doctors help people every two minutes on average in the Australian Outback! They have over 60 airplanes. In 2017, the planes flew more than 26 million kilometers. That's like 34 trips to the moon and back!

Sometimes the planes can land on small airstrips near farms, but sometimes there are no airstrips, so they have to land on flat land or highways. The farmers and their friends light these temporary runways with their car head lights if it's dark. If the sick person needs special treatment or an operation, the plane becomes a flying ambulance. The doctors and nurses put the patient in the plane and fly the patient to the nearest hospital.

3 Complete the sentences.

car   hospitals   patients   plane   highways

1   The problem with being sick in the Outback is there aren't any doctors or _____ .

2   That is why doctors fly in to see _____ .

3   The Flying Doctor's planes need to land on airstrips, _____ , or flat land.

4   When there is no proper runway and it is nighttime, people use their _____ headlights to light the runway.

5   When people have to go to the hospital, they use the Flying Doctor's _____ as an ambulance.

4 🎧 017 Listen and circle the correct option.

1   Robin Miller was

   a   a doctor.   b   a nurse.

2   She

   a   could fly a plane.   b   could not fly a plane.

3   Aboriginal children

   a   had all their vaccinations.   b   did not have all their vaccinations.

4   Robin Miller flew

   a   influenza vaccines to the Outback.   b   polio vaccines to the Outback.

5   She put the vaccine on

   a   sugar cubes.   b   cookies.

5 Think about the last time you were sick and answer the questions.

1   Where did you go?

_____

2   Who did you see?

_____

3   How did you get there?

_____

4   How long did it take to get there?

_____

5   Have you ever been to the hospital?

_____

I know about the Australian Outback.

3 Hanging out

> How can we plan a festival?

1 Listen and complete the sentences with a word from the box.

baskeball   skateboards   helmet   bike   scooter

1   I rode to the park on my _____ yesterday.

2   Two teams were playing _____ on the court in the park.

3   One of our classmates had a brand new _____ with her. She went very fast.

4   We stopped and watched the children use their _____ on the new ramp.

5   Oh, no! That girl didn't have her _____ on. I hope she's OK.

2 Look and write the sport.

CODE CRACKER

_____ court

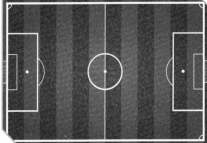

_____ field

_____ court

3 Play *I'm thinking of a word* in groups of four. One person chooses a word from the box in 1. The others ask questions to guess what it is.

Does it have wheels?

Yes, it does.

Do you push it with your feet?

Yes, you do.

Is it a scooter?

Yes, it is.

A beach festival

VOCABULARY

I will learn words for free-time activities.

1 Look and write.

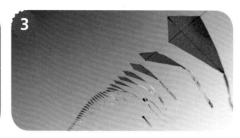

2 Read and complete.

It was Victor's birthday and his uncle Jim gave him a kite, but Victor doesn't like **1** _____ kites. His aunt bought him a **2** _____ to a pop concert to see a famous band, but Victor doesn't like **3** _____ to concerts either. Victor's dad took him ten-pin **4** _____ for his birthday and then invited him to a pizza **5** _____ . Victor loves **6** _____ at restaurants.

3 Listen and check your answers to 2.

4 Listen and label the pictures.

knee pads   saddle   riding hat
elbow pads   riding boots   helmet

1 _____

2 _____

3 _____

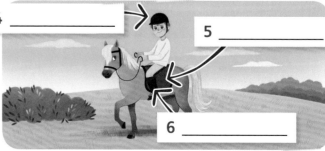

4 _____

5 _____

6 _____

I can use words for free-time activities.

Language lab

GRAMMAR: FIXED FUTURE PLANS

I will talk about fixed plans for the future.

1 Put the words in order and write sentences.

1 festival / ice-skating / tomorrow. / going / We're / an / to

_____

2 ice-skaters / Some / Olympic / doing / are / show / a

_____

3 too / We're / skates / our / taking / with us

_____

4 at / two o'clock / starting / The / show / is / tomorrow afternoon.

_____

5 finishing / It / until / isn't / o'clock / tomorrow. / five

_____

2 Read and complete. Use the verbs in brackets.

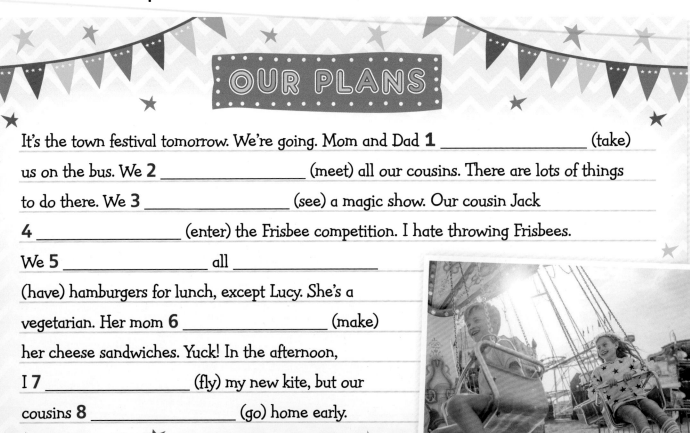

OUR PLANS

It's the town festival tomorrow. We're going. Mom and Dad **1** _____ (take) us on the bus. We **2** _____ (meet) all our cousins. There are lots of things to do there. We **3** _____ (see) a magic show. Our cousin Jack **4** _____ (enter) the Frisbee competition. I hate throwing Frisbees. We **5** _____ all _____ (have) hamburgers for lunch, except Lucy. She's a vegetarian. Her mom **6** _____ (make) her cheese sandwiches. Yuck! In the afternoon, I **7** _____ (fly) my new kite, but our cousins **8** _____ (go) home early.

3 Number the sentences in order. Then listen and check.

☐ He's meeting his friend David there to prepare the horses.

☐ Howie is very excited. `I`

☐ After riding, they are going to David's house for lunch.

☐ He's going to the stables at 10 o'clock.

☐ Why? Tomorrow morning he's going horseback riding.

☐ What an exciting day!

☐ And after that they are watching a movie together.

☐ Then after lunch, they are playing video games.

4 Look at the agenda and write down Chloe's plans.

10:00	go to my dance class
12:00	watch my favorite program on TV
1:30	have lunch with Grandma and Grandpa
3:00	make cookies with Mom
6:00	play video games with Harry

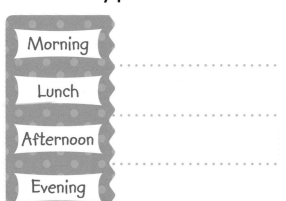

Next Saturday at ten o'clock Chloe's going _____

_____

_____

_____

5 Design a timetable for your Saturday plans.

Morning ....

Lunch ....

Afternoon ....

Evening

6 Ask and answer with a partner about plans.

What are you doing on Saturday morning?

I'm going horseback riding. What about you?

I can talk about fixed plans for the future.

Story lab

READING

I will read a story about a birthday.

Hiroki's birthday

1 **Read *Hiroki's Birthday* again and circle T (True) or F (False).**

1	It was Taro's birthday.	T / F
2	Hiroki's mom woke him up in the morning.	T / F
3	Hiroki found a note from his granddad in the yard.	T / F
4	Hiroki went to play basketball with Taro.	T / F
5	Hiroki listened to his favorite band all alone.	T / F
6	Everybody forgot Hiroki's birthday.	T / F

2 **Correct the false statements from 1.**

_____

_____

_____

3 **Find words or phrases in the story that mean the same.**

1   a bad beginning   _____

2   perhaps   _____

3   suppose   _____

4   the person who serves in a restaurant   _____

5   excited about something that's going to happen   _____

4 **Write the punctuation for direct speech. Check the story on page 48 of your Student's Book.**

1   _____ Are you going to the skate park today _____ Taro _____ _____ he asked _____

2   Keiko asked _____ _____ Are you looking forward to it _____ _____

3   _____ I can't wait _____ _____ said Hiroki _____ _____ Thank you everyone _____ _____

5 Complete the conversation for you. Then act it out with your friend.

Your friend: Go on! Open the box!

You: _____

Your friend: Yes! It's for you.

You: _____

Your friend: What is it?

You: _____

6 Write your opinion of the story.

Key

1 = very bad
5 = very good

My opinion

My favorite character is _____ .

My favorite part is _____ .

I think the story is interesting / funny / scary / silly .

I liked / didn't like the story because _____ .

I think it's _____ story. I _____ and

_____ .

① ② ③ ④ ⑤

7 Ask and answer with a partner.

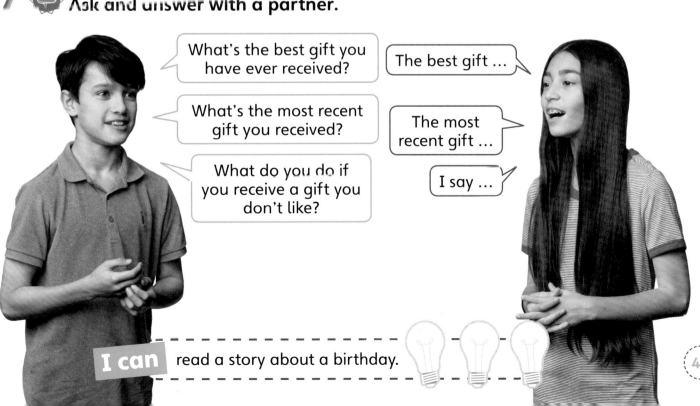

What's the best gift you have ever received?

The best gift …

What's the most recent gift you received?

The most recent gift …

What do you do if you receive a gift you don't like?

I say …

I can read a story about a birthday.

Experiment lab

MATH: PARTITIONING IN SPORTS

1 **Look at the shapes and follow the instructions.**

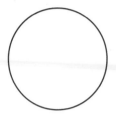

circle

Divide into sixths.

square

Divide in half.

rectangle

Divide into quarters.

2 **Read and color the fractions.**

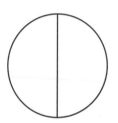    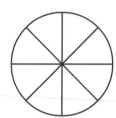

a one-half   **b** two-fourths   **c** two-thirds   **d** five-sixths   **e** four-eighths   **f** three-sixths

____   ____   ____   ____   ____   ____

3 **Read and write the fractions.**

How to write FRACTIONS

Imagine you have an apple pie. Eight people want a slice, so you are going to cut eight slices. Now imagine you take the first slice from that pie. That slice is one eighth of the apple pie.

When you write a fraction, the top number is the slice you took from the apple pie, the bottom number is the total number of slices.

1/8 is how you write that fraction.

Now think of making slices for different numbers of children. Write the fraction for each.

1 Slices for 3 children: _____

2 Slices for 5 children: _____

3 Slices for 7 children: _____

4 **Now write the number fractions under the words in 3.**

EXPERIMENT TIME

Report

1 Look at the information on the soccer practice card. Write the results in full.

		Number of attempts at goal	Number of goals
1	Derek	4	1
2	Samantha	3	2
3	Fred	5	3
4	Hetty	2	1
5	Mike	8	5

1 *Derek scored one quarter of the times he tried.* _____

2 _____

3 _____

4 _____

5 _____

2 Look at the cake, read, and solve the math problems.

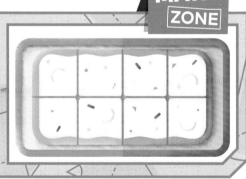

MATH ZONE

Yesterday, Grandma made a cake. She always makes rectangular cakes. She made a rectangular one yesterday, too. She cut the cake into eighths.

She gave one slice to Arabella and another to Grandpa. Arabella divided her slice into two halves and shared it with her baby brother. How much of the whole cake did Arabella have?

_____

When it was time to go home, Grandma gave Arabella half of the remaining cake to take home with her. How much of the cake was left for the next day?

_____

3 Reflect on fractions.

Do you find writing fractions easy or difficult? _____

Do you think understanding fractions is a useful skill?

_____

Have you used fractions outside the classroom? _____

I know about partitioning and fractions.

When is it happening?

COMMUNICATION: TIME PHRASES

I will talk about when things are happening.

1 Work in pairs. Ask and answer.

What time is it?

It's quarter past two.

2 Look at 1. Write the times in words.

1   It's _____ .
2   _____
3   _____
4   _____
5   _____
6   _____
7   _____
8   _____

3 Listen and write the times.

Getting up at _____

Swimming class starts at _____

Swimming class ends at _____

Mom picks me up at _____

Hair cut at _____

Back for lunch at _____

4 In pairs, ask and answer about Helen's Saturday morning.

What's she doing at 11:00?

She's having her hair cut at 11:00.

5 What are you doing next Saturday?

SATURDAY ★ ★ ★
· ....
· ....
· ....
· ....
· ....

6 Ask and answer with your partner. Fill in their schedule.

SATURDAY ★ ★ ★
· ....
· ....
· ....
· ....

I can talk about when things are happening.

Writing lab

I will write an email about future plans.

AN EMAIL ABOUT FUTURE PLANS

1 **Complete the email with the correct form of the words in brackets.**

To: Sophia H.   **Subject:** Invitation!

Hi Sophia,

I **1** _____ (go) to a national park next week with some friends from my running team. Do you want to come? This is the plan: We **2** _____ (meet) at school in the morning. We are going by bus.

First, we **3** _____ (eat) lunch together indoors in the cafeteria. Then we're playing some outdoor games. Next, we **4** _____ (run) around the lake. You love running – you must come! After that, I **5** _____ (play) volleyball on the red team until dinner. Finally, we **6** _____ (watch) a movie in the evening. We **7** _____ (not/come) back early. We'll get home around 11 p.m. Is that OK?

Elena

---

2 **Read the email in 1 again and answer the questions.**

1 What's Elena doing next week? _____

2 Who is she going with? _____ _____

3 How are they getting there? _____

4 What are they doing there? _____

_____

5 Are they coming back early? _____

3 **Write an email asking a friend to join you at a planned event. Tell them the plan.**

_____
_____
_____
_____
_____

I can write an email about future plans.

47

PROJECT AND REVIEW UNIT 3

Design you own festival

Project report

1 Complete for your festival.

What kind of festival did you design?		What did the plan include?	
☐ book	☐ music	☐ activities	☐ places for activities
☐ street sports	☐ sports	☐ where to eat	☐ bathrooms
☐ dance	☐ _____	☐ entrance	☐ _____
What did your brochure include?		**What did your class think about it?**	
☐ description of events	☐ time of events	☐ They liked it.	☐ They asked questions.
☐ description of food	☐ time for lunch	☐ They made suggestions.	
☐ _____		☐ _____	

2 Complete your project report.

OUR FESTIVAL: _____

What kind of festival did you design?

We designed _____

_____ .

What did your brochure include?

It included _____

_____ .

What did the plan include?

It included _____

_____ .

What did your class think about it?

They _____

_____ .

3 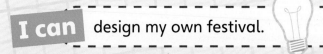 Share your report with a partner. Ask questions.

I can design my own festival.

1 Complete the phrases. Write go, play, or ride.

1 _____ your scooter

2 _____ your skateboard

3 _____ roller-skating

4 _____ baseball

5 _____ horseback riding

6 _____ Frisbee

7 _____ volleyball

8 _____ bowling

2 🔊 023 Listen and check ☑ the correct agenda, A or B.

A

Saturday	Sunday
8:00 a.m. get up	6:00 p.m. homework
9:15 a.m. play volleyball	
11:00 a.m. Molly picks up	
1:00 p.m. go bowling	☐

B

Saturday	Sunday
8:00 a.m. get up	8:00 p.m. homework
9:15 a.m. play volleyball	
11:00 a.m. Holly picks up	
1:00 p.m. go bowling	☐

3 Put the words in order and write sentences.

1 baseball / am playing / at half past five this evening. / I

_____

2 with my mom / I / to the supermarket / am going / between six / and seven o'clock.

_____

3 to school / I / am traveling / by bus today.

_____

4 am going / I / at half past nine. / to bed

_____

4 Complete the sentences for future plans.

1 I _____ (not/play) Frisbee tomorrow.

2 We _____ (play) basketball later today.

3 Who _____ (you/come) to the school concert with this evening?

4 She _____ (go) bowling this afternoon.

5 They _____ (not/watch) TV tonight.

Now go to your Progress Chart on page 4.

4 Movie magic

How can we make a movie trailer?

1 **Read the descriptions. Write the words.**

> actor   camera   director   movie   scene

1   This is the equipment used to film a movie.   _____

2   This is part of a movie or a short piece of action.   _____

3   This is the person on screen who acts in a movie.   _____

4   This is something you see at the movie theater.   _____

5   This is the person who tells the actors what to do.   _____

2 **Complete the information about the movie. Use the words from 1.**

1   This year's big _____ was about a princess in a glass castle.

2   In one _____ , the princess dramatically rescued the horses.

3   The _____ won an award for making the movie.

4   The director said the _____ worked hard and listened to him.

5   It was difficult to take the _____ to the mountains to film the outdoor scenes.

3 🔊 024 **Listen and check the answers to 2.**

4 💡 **Number the pictures in order. Then describe them to a partner.**

CODE CRACKER ⚙️⚙️

Amazing movies

VOCABULARY

I will learn words to talk about movies.

1 Read and sort. Use a dictionary to help you.

> frightening   sound effects   scene   animation   interesting   music

sight	sound	feelings
_____ _____	_____ _____	_____ _____

2 Read and match.

1   What kind of movies do you like?
2   What's your favorite movie?
3   What's it about?
4   What's your favorite scene?
5   Who's your favorite actor?

a   It's about a magical nanny.
b   I like musicals.
c   My favorite actor is Emily Blunt.
d   I like the scene in the park best.
e   It's *Mary Poppins Returns*.

3 In pairs, ask and answer the questions in 2.

4 Listen and label the pictures. What are they watching?

> a horror film   a comedy   a 3D film

_____

_____

5 **Ph** Complete the sentences with -tion and -ph. Then say.

The dol_____in laughed at the anima_____ on its _____one.

Language lab

GRAMMAR: MAKING COMPARISONS

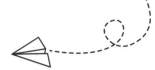

I will compare things.

1 Read the movie reviews and write the titles.

> A Dog's Paradise   Miss Kate's Mystery in Texas   The Finders   Police Patrol

My Movie Review

1 _____ ★★★★★

This is the year's best movie for people who like a good mystery. It's better than the last movie set in Mississippi. The special effects are great. There are a lot of explosions because the mystery is set in an oil field. This makes it the most frightening and exciting movie in the series.

2 _____ ★★★★★

This is a smart, interesting, and exciting movie. It's about two middle school students and an epidemic in their school that is turning students into zombies. The students use their science skills to find the cure to the Zombie disease. The acting, the script, and the special effects are amazing.

3 _____ ★★★★★

This is one of the funniest movies I've ever seen. It is full of great jokes and the acting is hilarious. It is about a police officer who loves his patrol car. When someone steals his car, he must go through many crazy and funny experiences to get it back. You'll love it!

4 _____ ★★★★★

This is the worst movie I have ever seen in my life. I love dogs and I usually love any movie with a dog in it, but they don't use real dogs. They use computer generated dogs and it's awful. It isn't funny and I think it's supposed to be a comedy. Don't see it!

2 Read 1 again and answer the questions.

1 Which movie is the most frightening?
_____

2 Which movie is the funniest?
_____

3 Which movie is the worst?
_____

4 Which movie is the smartest?
_____

3 In pairs, write a short song or chant for one of the movies in 1.

*Two science kids in a lab,
Doing experiments,
Finding a cure!
Two science kids in a lab,
Where are they now?*

_____
_____
_____
_____

4 Read and circle T (True) or F (False). Then correct the false statements.

What is the most expensive movie ever made? Is it *Star Wars: The Rise of Skywalker*? It cost $275 million. Is it *Avengers: Endgame*? It cost $356 million. No-one really knows because Hollywood doesn't say. It's a secret.

Which is the most popular movie of all time? Is *Star Wars* more popular than *Avengers*? No, 100 million people saw *Avengers* the first weekend. 46 million people saw *Star Wars* the first weekend. Our expert critic said, "They are both wonderful movies. You must see them. *Star Wars* is more frightening than *Avengers* and *Avengers* is funnier than *Star Wars*."

So, *Avengers* is the biggest movie and it's the most expensive, but is it better? What do you think? Which one do you like? Which one is more interesting? Which one is funnier? Which one is more frightening?

1	*Avengers* wasn't as expensive as *Star Wars*.	T / F	_____
2	*Avengers* was more popular than *Star Wars*.	T / F	_____
3	*Avengers* isn't as funny as *Star Wars*.	T / F	_____
4	*Star Wars* isn't as frightening as *Avengers*.	T / F	_____

5 Solve the math problems about the movies in 4.

MATH ZONE

a What's the difference in revenue?

356 − 275 = _____ million dollars

b What's the combined revenue?

356 + 275 = _____ million dollars

c What's the total viewing audience?

100 + 46 = _____ million viewers

6 Think of an actor you like and an actor you don't like. Write their names in the bubbles. Then write sentences to compare them.

A I like [_____].

B I don't like [_____].

_____ is better than

_____. _____ isn't

as interesting as _____.

Values Listen to other people's opinions.

7 In pairs, talk about the actors you chose in 6. Respond to opinions.

 I can compare two or more things.

Story lab

I will read a story about two children who love movies.

A LUCKY DAY

1 Match to make phrases from the story *A Lucky Day*.

1	watch	a	on the ground
2	drop something	b	in the store
3	keep	c	the money
4	turn	d	a movie
5	the most expensive toy	e	around

2 Read and circle T (True) or F (False).

1 William and Betty's family were rich.   T / F
2 They saw a toy in the store that cost too much money.   T / F
3 A well-dressed man was early for a movie.   T / F
4 He entered the building without realizing he dropped something.   T / F

3 Who said it? Write *Betty*, *William*, or *Max*.

1 _____   "Look, Betty! It goes around and you can see the pictures moving."
2 _____   "Yes! But it's the most expensive toy in the store!"
3 _____   "I'd love to watch a movie."
4 _____   "Thank you! The money isn't as important as the papers."

4 Complete the sentences.

excited   generous   honest   lucky   poor

1 William and Betty are _____ because they could go to a movie.
2 William and Betty are _____ because they gave the man his money and papers.
3 William and Betty are _____ because their family doesn't have a lot of money.
4 William and Betty are _____ because they met a famous director.
5 Max Chapman is _____ because he gave the children the money.

5 Compare yourself to the characters.

I'm not as honest as William and Betty.

I'm as excited about movies as William and Betty.

1 _____   2 _____

3 _____   4 _____

5 _____

6 Answer for you. Then ask and answer with a partner.

1 You're looking at a toy. What toy are you looking at?

_____

2 You want to see a movie. What movie do you want to see?

_____

3 You find some money on the ground? What do you do?

_____

4 Someone gives you a money prize. What do you do with the money?

_____

5 You meet a famous director. What do you say?

_____

7 Think of a movie you want to see soon. Read and check ☑.

1 Do you think the movie will be exciting?

I hope so. ☐   I hope not. ☐

2 Do you think there will be any popcorn?

I hope so. ☐   I hope not. ☐

3 Do you think you will like the movie?

I hope so. ☐   I hope not. ☐

4 Do you think the tickets will be expensive?

I hope so. ☐   I hope not. ☐

5 Do you think the theater will be crowded?

I hope so. ☐   I hope not. ☐

6 Do you think your friends will want to see it with you?

I hope so. ☐   I hope not. ☐

I can read a story about two children who love movies.

I will find out how an animation loop works.

1 Read the article *Moving Pictures* again. Then answer in full sentences.

1 What's one image in a movie called?

_____

2 How many frames does a movie have?

_____

3 How did animators create movies in the past?

_____

4 How do animators make animations now?

_____

5 What is a repeated sequence of frames called?

_____

2 Complete the chart.

animation drawing create enjoy
imagination remember repetition

action word (verb)	thing (noun)
imagine	1 imagination
2 _____	memory
animate	3 _____
4 _____	enjoyment
draw	5 _____
6 _____	creation
repeat	7 _____

3 Read and solve the math problems. Show your work.

MATH ZONE

1 The movie starts at 3:30. It's an hour and a half long. What time does it finish?

_____ ☐

2 The actor is 25 years old. The movie takes four years to make. How old is the actor at the end of filming?

_____ ☐

3 34 million people saw the movie *Benjamin Rabbit* the first weekend. 22 million people saw the movie *Sandtown* the first weekend. How many more people saw *Benjamin Rabbit* than *Sandtown*?

_____ ☐

EXPERIMENT TIME

Report

1 Complete the chart. Then share your ideas with a partner.

Things I drew to create an action sequence on a phenakistoscope
A person jumping.

2 Read the example. Then write your own report.

DID THE PHENAKISTOSCOPE WORK?

I drew a person jumping on the paper and attached it to the phenakistoscope. First, I spun it slowly and it didn't work. Then I spun the phenakistoscope quickly, but my eye was too far away from the slit and it didn't work.
I had to try about five times to make it work. My biggest problem was getting my eye in the right position to see the image.
Finally, I saw the person jumping. Next time, I will draw the pictures more carefully, so the loop looks smoother.

DID THE PHENAKISTOSCOPE WORK?

I drew _____ on the paper and attached it to the phenakistoscope. First, I spun it _____ and _____ . Then I spun the phenakistoscope _____ but _____ .
I had to try about _____ times to make it work. My biggest problem was _____ . Finally, I saw _____ . Next time, I will _____ _____ .

3 Talk about your report with a partner.

 how an animation loop works.

Movie makers

COMMUNICATION: WHAT MIGHT HAPPEN?

I will talk about what might happen.

1 Unscramble the words and label the pictures.

TERWRI

UNSOD ENGEERIN

ETXARS

ADUINECE

ISPCTR

TPEORS

2 Read and complete the conversation.

> That would be great!   We might see another dance.   It might be a musical.

Man: They're making a movie in the town square.

Woman: Really? What kind of movie?

Man: _____
I saw some actors dancing.

Woman: I hope so. Musicals are my favorite movies.

Man: Let's go and watch the filming.
_____

Woman: Yes, and we might be able to work as extras!

Man: _____

3 Listen and check. Then act out the conversation.

4 Work in pairs. You are making a movie. Say your three biggest worries.

> We might not find any good actors.

> We might have a terrible director.

I can talk about what might happen.

Writing lab

A MOVIE REVIEW

I will write a movie review.

1 Write the names of three movies you have seen recently and color the stars.

Movie title	Rating
1	☆ ☆ ☆ ☆ ☆
2	☆ ☆ ☆ ☆ ☆
3	☆ ☆ ☆ ☆ ☆

2 Choose one movie from **1** and write what happens.

_____

_____

_____

_____

3 Make a poster for the movie you wrote about in **2**. Include the following:

Live action or animation?	
Number of actors	
Names of two main characters	
Who will or might enjoy it?	

4 Read the example. Then write a review of the movie.

- What's it about?
- What's your opinion of the movie?
- Why did you like it?
- Who would like it?

I recently saw *The Dragomads*. It was great and I recommend it to anyone who likes animated movies about animals. It's about a group of homeless dragons who travel the world looking for the best place to live. I liked it because the story was original and exciting. I think it's a good movie for anyone from eight to twelve years old. I give it four stars.

_____

_____

_____

I can write a movie review.

Make a movie trailer

Project report

1 Think about your movie trailer and answer the questions.

What kinds of trailers did you watch for research?	What movie did you choose to make a trailer for?
_____ _____ _____ _____	_____
	Which three scenes did you choose? _____ _____
Who took these roles?	**What part of your trailer was difficult to make?**
director: _____ camera operator: _____ actors: _____	_____ _____
voice-over: _____ sound effects: _____	**Did you need to make changes to your storyboard or script?** _____
music: _____	**What feedback did you get about your trailer?** _____

2 Write up your project report using the answers in 1.

Project report – Make a movie trailer

_____

_____

_____

_____

3 Share your report with a partner. Ask questions.

I can make a movie trailer.

1 Circle words in the word snake.

famoussceneactordirectormoviefrighteningsoundeffectsscriptanimationexpensivecharactersciencefiction

2 Complete with words from the word snake.

Steven Spielberg is a very famous **1** _____ . His **2** _____ include *E.T. The Extra-Terrestrial* (1982) and *Jurassic Park* (1993). These are **3** _____ _____ movies. *Jurassic Park* is about an imagined natural world and *E.T.* is about an alien stuck on Earth. *Jurassic Park* is scarier than *E.T.*

E.T. is one of Spielberg's most loved characters. He doesn't talk much, but he has one of the most **4** _____ lines in movie history, "E.T. phone home." The **5** _____ where he says that line is filmed in Elliot's sister's bedroom. If you want to read the **6** _____ for *E.T* you can find it on the internet.

The actors in *E.T.* were children. The **7** _____ of Elliot was ten years old. Henry Thomas played Elliot, and Elliot's sister, Gertie, was played by Drew Barrymore, who is now one of the most famous **8** _____ in Hollywood.

3 Complete the chart.

funnier	the funniest
better	**1** _____
2 _____	the worst
3 _____	the most interesting
more famous	**4** _____
more frightening	**5** _____
6 _____	the most exciting

4 Read and circle the correct words.

Boy: It **1** might / might not rain. Let's go to the movie and not the park.

Girl: The movie **2** might / might not have good sound effects. It's about extra-terrestrials on Earth.

Boy: I don't know. It **3** might / might not be interesting. Alan said it was boring.

Girl: Hmm. What else can we see? Oh, this movie **4** might / might not be good. It's about a lost dog that travels thousands of kilometers to get home.

Boy: It **5** might / might not be sad. You'd better take a tissue.

Girl: Wait. I **6** might / might not have enough money.

Now go to your Progress Chart on page 4.

2 Checkpoint
UNITS 3 AND 4

1 🎧 027 **Listen and follow Ben's path.**

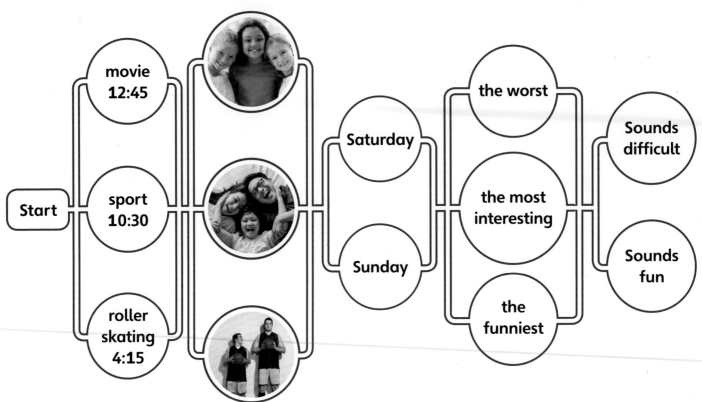

2 **Look at and listen to 1 again. Circle the best answer.**

1 Who is Ben playing basketball with on Saturday morning?

    a   his family   **b**   his teammates

2 Does Ben like windy weather?

    a   Yes, he does.   **b**   No, he doesn't.

3 What's he doing on Sunday?

    a   He's doing a fun project.   **b**   He's doing a boring project.

4 What kind of movies are the worst according to the girl?

    a   animation   **b**   horror

3 🎧 028 **Listen and follow Kelly's path in 1.**

4 Read the review of the movie Kelly saw and answer the questions.

★ ★ ★ ★ ★ *Lucas at Work* **is a fantastic live action comedy movie.**

By Kelly Smith – July 18

It's the funniest movie this year! The main character is called Lucas Delucia. The actor who plays him is Cameron Buttersworth. He's my favorite actor because I think he's really good at doing funny scenes.

At the beginning of the movie, Lucas meets a group of neighborhood kids who want to solve an old town mystery. They are all bored because they have nothing to do over the summer. All the characters in the film are very silly and very funny. I love the movie because lots of interesting and crazy things happen. The special effects are amazing, too. The best part is when the mayor is chasing them down the street on a scooter.

I think children, teenagers, and adults will love this movie.

1   What is the movie called? _____

2   What kind of movie is it? _____

3   Does Kelly like the movie? How do you know? _____

4   What words describe the characters? _____

5   Who would enjoy the movie? _____

5 Write a review of a movie you've seen.

live action   animation   science fiction   funny   scary   interesting
exciting   director   sound effects   special effects   characters

_____

_____

_____

_____

6 Talk about what you're doing on Saturday and Sunday with a partner.

What are you doing on Saturday?

I'm playing baseball with my teammates.

1 🎧 029 Listen to the conversation and answer the questions.

1 What are the children talking about?

_____

2 What was the girl crazy about before?

_____

3 What does she like now?

_____

4 What does the boy like about his choice?

_____

2 Read and answer the questions.

ANIME

Anime cartoons are famous all over the world. "Anime" is the Japanese word for animations. Anime characters usually resemble real people. They have large eyes and are very expressive. Landscapes are important, too. When a character is angry, the landscape reflects this: the sky turns purple along with the character's hair and eyes! When a character is happy, the sky is bright and clear.

To make anime, Japanese artists create hand-drawn pictures in black and white. Each picture is called a frame. The artists put the frames together. Then the pictures are put onto a computer and digitally colored.

To draw 60 to 90 seconds of cartoon takes an anime artist about six weeks. We can often see Anime episodes on TV. Each episode lasts 24 minutes and needs 34,560 frames! So next time you see an Anime clip, think of all the hard work behind it.

1 Where does "Anime" come from?

Anime comes from _____.

2 What do Anime characters usually look like?

Anime characters _____.

3 Why is color so important in Anime cartoons?

Color _____.

4 What is special about the way the artists create the drawings?

The artists _____.

3 Interview six people to find out which TV cartoons they like best.

Name	Favorite cartoon	What do you like about it?
1		
2		
3		
4		
5		
6		

4 Write about a popular cartoon in your country. What is it about? Who are the central characters? Where do they live? What do they do?

5 In groups, invent a cartoon character. Think about what is special about the character. Draw a picture of your cartoon character. Look at the Ideas Box below.

Can your character fly?
Is it strong?
Is it an animal?
Where does it live?
What does it do?

6 In the same groups, write a short story with your ideas from 5.

I know about Sakura and Japanese anime.

Once in a lifetime

How can we plan the trip of a lifetime?

1 Label the pictures.

mountain   subway   helicopter   lake   train   pilot

2 Unscramble the words and complete.

I live in the city. I travel to school by
1 _____ (BYWSUA). There are
2 _____ (NDWIOSW), but there is no
3 _____ (VWEI) because you are in a
tunnel. All you can see are black walls. It's
very 4 _____ (NISOY). It makes a loud
sound that hurts my ears, but I don't mind
because it's fast. I think it is the best way
to 5 _____ (TERAVL) when you are in
a city.

3 Listen and check the answers to 2.

4 Complete using the code.

CODE CRACKER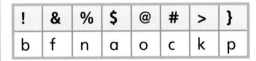

!	&	%	$	@	#	>	}
b	f	n	a	o	c	k	p

1   Be careful when you get @% and
    @&& the train in the subway.

    _____ _____

2   Don't wear your !$#>}$#>.
    Take it @&& and carry it.

    _____ _____

Let's explore!

VOCABULARY

I will learn words to talk about travel experiences.

1  Read and sort.

go camping   go up a mountain   go snorkeling   visit a palace
climb up a tower   ride a camel   feed the penguins   see a hummingbird
fly in a helicopter   fly in a hot-air balloon   stay in a hotel

on land	in the ocean	in the air	with animals

2 Read the clues and circle the activity.

1 The air is fresh. There are trees and there's a dirt path. My legs are tired.
   a I'm traveling by subway.
   b I'm flying in a hot-air balloon.
   c I'm hiking up a mountain.

2 We go up suddenly. Now we move forwards. We're in the air. It's very noisy.
   a We're climbing up a tower.
   b We're flying in a helicopter.
   c We're snorkeling.

3 Ask and answer with a partner.

1 Would you like to stay in a hotel or go camping?
2 Would you prefer to ride a camel or feed the penguins?
3 Would you like to visit a palace or see a hummingbird?
4 Would you rather go snorkeling or fly in a hot-air balloon?

4 Ph 031 Write the words in the chart based on the end sounds /s/, /z/, or /iz/. Then listen, check, and repeat.

backpacks   boxes   buses   camels
cars   donkeys   mountains   palaces
suitcases   tents

/s/	/z/	/iz/

I can use words to talk about travel experiences.

Language lab

GRAMMAR: TALKING ABOUT LIFE EXPERIENCES

I will talk about experiences I've had in my life.

1 Write the correct form of the verbs in brackets.

Have you ever ...

1 _____ (climb) a climbing wall at a gym?

2 _____ (hike) in a national park?

3 _____ (stay) in a cabin?

4 _____ (fly) in a plane?

5 _____ (ride) horse?

6 _____ (see) a horror movie?

7 _____ (feed) the ducks in the park?

2 Ask and answer the questions in 1.

Have you ever climbed a climbing wall at a gym?

Yes, I have. / No, I haven't.

3 Read and complete the things that Lilian has and hasn't done.

Lilian loves going on vacation. She's been hiking lots of times, but she's never **1** _____ (climb up) a tower and she's never **2** _____ (visit) a palace. She's never **3** _____ (go) camping either. But next summer she and her family are going to go to Ireland to do all of that!

In Ireland they will travel by car and by train. Lilian has traveled by car, bus, and taxi but she's never **4** _____ (travel) by train.

They will visit the Dublin Zoo to feed the penguins. Lilian has never **5** _____ (feed) penguins before, but she has **6** _____ (ride) a camel and she has **7** _____ (see) a hummingbird.

4 Look at the chart and complete the questions and answers.

Tell us about your experiences.	Kim	Karen	Helena	Andrew	Morris
hike up a mountain	no	yes	no	yes	yes
travel by boat	no	no	no	yes	no
visit a palace	yes	yes	yes	yes	no
ride a camel	no	no	yes	yes	no
see a hummingbird	yes	yes	yes	no	yes
fly in a helicopter	no	yes	no	no	yes
feed a deer	yes	no	no	no	yes
stay in a tent	no	yes	no	yes	yes

1 ___Has___ Karen ___hiked___ up a mountain?   ___Yes, she has.___

2 _____ Andrew _____ by boat?   _____

3 _____ Helena and Andrew _____ a palace?   _____

4 _____ Kim ever _____ a camel?   _____

5 _____ Helena and Morris _____ a hummingbird? _____

6 _____ Andrew ever _____ in a helicopter? _____

7 _____ Kim and Morris _____ a deer?   _____

8 _____ Kim _____ in a tent?   _____

9 _____ Andrew and Morris _____ in a tent? _____

5 Talk about what the people in 4 have and haven't done.

> Has Helena ever gone camping?

> No, she hasn't.

6 Write three things from this lesson you've done and three things you've never done.

I've _____ .   I've never _____ .

I've _____ .   I've never _____ .

I've _____ .   I've never _____ .

7 Tell your partner about your lists in 6.

> I've stayed in a tent.

> I've never fed a deer.

I can talk about experiences I've had in my life.

Story lab

READING

I will read a fable about two travelers.

The travelers and the bear, by Aesop

1 🔧 **Read *The travelers and the bear* again. Then number the events in order.**

a   The man lay down on the ground. ☐

b   The woman asked him what the bear had said. ☐

c   Two travelers were on a journey around the world. ☐ 1

d   They heard a terrible roar. ☐

e   The bear whispered to the man. ☐

f   The woman ran to a tree and climbed up it. ☐

2 Complete with *woman*, *man*, or *bear*.

A **1** _____ and a **2** _____ were hiking through a forest. Suddenly, they heard a terrible roar and screamed. The **3** _____ ran to a tree and climbed up. The **4** _____ remembered an interesting fact. The **5** _____ could feel the **6** _____'s sharp claws and soft fur. The **7** _____'s heart was beating fast. After a moment, the **8** _____ walked away. "Was the **9** _____ talking to you?" the **10** _____ asked. And the **11** _____ walked on, a wiser man.

3 Read and solve the math problems.

MATH ZONE

1   A brown bear eats 35 kilograms of food a day. How much food does it eat in five days? _____

2   A brown bear weights 310 kilograms before hibernation. It weighs half that after hibernation. How much does it weigh after hibernation? _____

3   A brown bear enters its den at the end of October and stays for six months. When does it come out? _____

4 **Read the title of Aesop's fable and circle what you think you think the fable is about. Then skim the story and check.**

THE DOG AND THE BONE

I think it's about ...

a a crow that likes to sing.   b a clever fox.   c a greedy dog.   d a race.

5 **Read the fable and write the moral.**

One day a butcher gave a hungry dog a nice meaty bone. The dog was very happy as it walked away carrying the bone in its mouth. The dog walked a short distance until it reached a bridge. It stopped at the center of the bridge and started its feast. Suddenly, it looked down into the water and saw another dog with a bone in its mouth. This other dog was looking up with angry eyes.
The greedy dog thought, "I want my bone and that bone, too." The dog opened its mouth to bark at the dog in the water. As soon as the dog opened its mouth, the bone fell with a splash into the stream. The dog jumped into the stream, but of course, there was no dog in the water and no bone either.
In fact, the dog now had no bone. Its bone was at the bottom of the stream and the other bone was nothing but a reflection!

The moral of the fable is

_____

_____

6 **Create a cartoon based on the fable *The Dog and the Bone*.**

I can   read a fable about two travelers.

Experiment lab

SCIENCE: ANIMALS AROUND THE WORLD

I will find out about different features of animals.

1 **Read the definitions and write the words.**

1   the hard pointed mouth of a bird   _____

2   a sharp curved nail on some animals' feet   _____

3   a large round shape that rises above the surface of something   _____

4   the part of a bird's or insect's body that it uses for flying   _____

5   the thick, soft hair that covers the bodies of some animals   _____

2 **Do the quiz. Circle a or b.**

Animal Quiz!

1 A porcupine has sharp needles on its body to

   a   protect it from predators.

   b   look attractive in the forest.

2 A porcupine's long claws help it

   a   run fast when in danger.

   b   find food in forests and deserts.

3 Thick hair on a camel's body keeps it

   a   colorful and bright.

   b   warm or cool.

4 Big, flat feet help a camel walk on

   a   sand.

   b   water.

5 Fat in the camel's humps provides _____ when there isn't any food.

   a   water

   b   energy

6 Hummingbirds live in

   a   Western and Eastern Europe.

   b   North and South America.

7 Hummingbirds are the _____ birds in the world.

   a   smallest

   b   biggest

8 Hummingbirds' wings move very fast, so they

   a   travel long distances and glide on the wind.

   b   stay in the same place for a long time.

3 Read, look, and match.

1 The pelican's beak expands to become a big spoon for collecting food. They eat fish.

2 The robin's beak is long and thin. It's shaped for digging in the ground and picking up worms.

3 Eagles' beaks are curved and strong. They eat small mammals like rabbits and they also eat fish.

4 Cardinals have short triangular beaks which are strong enough to break the hard shells of nuts and seeds.

EXPERIMENT TIME

Report

1 Write the tools you used as beaks. Use a dictionary if needed.

Tools we used as beaks	Tools that weren't useful
_____ _____ _____	_____ _____ _____

2 Tell your partner the tools that worked the best for the food you chose.

3 Write your report.

The best tools to use as beaks

_____

_____

_____

I know about the different features of animals.

At the tourist office

COMMUNICATION: ASKING FOR INFORMATION

I will ask for information.

1 Complete the conversation.

A: Excuse me, where can we see penguins?

B: You _____ do that at the beach. There's a bus tour from here.

A: Can we feed the penguins?

B: No, you _____ . It's not allowed. But you can watch the penguin parade. It's amazing.

A: How long does it take?

B: The tour is four hours _____ . The bus trip is an hour each way, and the penguin parade is two _____ long.

A: How much does it cost?

B: It's $35 for an adult and $15 for a _____ .

A: Great! I'd _____ two tickets, please.

B: Here you are. $50, please.

A: _____ you.

2 🎧 032 Listen and check the answers to 1.

3 💬 Read and complete. Then ask and answer about the tours.

Activity: See a koala

Where: Koala Park in the mountains near Sydney, Australia

Length of trip: ½ hour by bus from city, 3 hours to visit the park

Cost: Park entrance = $15 Bus ride = $7 per person

Activity: Feed the dolphins

Where:
_____
_____

Length of trip: _____
_____

Cost: _____

4 💬 In pairs, role-play buying tickets for the activities in 3.

Three return tickets to the Koala Park, please.

That's $21, please.

Here you are.

Thank you.

I can ask for information.

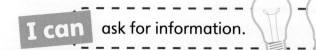

Writing lab

WRITING AN INTERVIEW

I will write an article about an interview.

1 Read the interview. Write the questions and match the photos.

Where are you now?   Why do you enjoy traveling?   Have you ever been to the desert?

Q: _____

A: Yes, I have. I went to the desert last year. It's the most amazing place in the world! I climbed a big sand dune. It was like a mountain of sand. It took six hours to travel across the desert from the road to the sand dune by camel.   Photo _____

Q: _____

A: I'm in the middle of the amazing country of Turkey! I'm traveling by bus to the town of Cappadocia from the capital city, Ankara. The hot-air balloons of Cappadocia fly every day at sunrise. It's beautiful! I want to take pictures from the air.   Photo _____

Q: _____

A: I enjoy traveling because I like visiting new places and I like meeting interesting people. I like taking photographs of amazing things.   Photo _____

2 Write another paragraph for the interview above.

Where would you like to go next?

I'd like to go _____ .

I've never _____ .

3 Make some flag bunting with countries you have visited or want to visit.

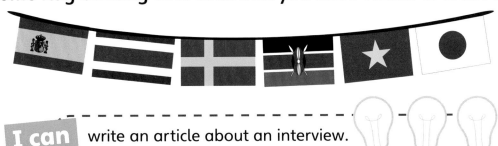

I can write an article about an interview.

Plan the trip of a lifetime

Project report

1 Complete for your group.

Things you have never done but would like to do	A country you would like to go to
_____ _____	_____ _____
Amazing experiences you can have there	**Places you marked on your chosen country's map**
_____ _____	_____ _____
Ways you will travel	**Information about each trip**
_____ _____	_____ _____

2 Complete your project report.

∿∿∿ Our trip of a lifetime ∿∿∿

Our group will go to the United States. We will start in Los Angeles. We will go to Disneyland in Anaheim. It takes about 50 minutes by bus from the airport to the park and costs $35 each. We have never been to California. From there, we will go to the San Diego Zoo ...

∿∿∿ Our trip of a lifetime ∿∿∿

3 Create a short video about your trip of a lifetime.

This is our trip of a lifetime.

I can plan the trip of a lifetime.

1 Unscramble and write the travel experiences.

1   RDIE A CAEML   _____

2   FYL NI A HTO-IAR BLAOLON   _____

3   OG MAGPCNI   _____

4   HIEK PU A MONUATIN   _____

2 Match to make questions.

1   How long   a   held a snake?

2   How much   b   go and see the pandas?

3   Where can we   c   does the tour take?

4   Have you ever   d   to do next?

5   What would you like   e   does the ticket cost?

3 Complete the questions and answers.

1   Q: _____ you _____
    a camel?

    A: Yes, I _____ .

2   Q: _____ you ever _____
    snorkeling?

    A: No, I _____ .

3   Q: _____ she _____ in
    a helicopter?

    A: No, she _____ .

4   Q: _____ they ever _____
    in a hotel?

    A: Yes, they _____ .

5   Q. _____ we _____ camping?

    A: Yes, we _____ .

4 Ask and answer.

Have you ever seen a hummingbird?

Have you gone snorkeling?

Do you prefer traveling by subway or by car?

Where would you like to go?

How much does a downtown tour in your city or town cost?

What would you like to do?

6 Codes and clues

> How and why do we use codes?

1 ⚙ Read the clues and write the words.

1 A mark made on the ground while walking in snow or mud. _____

2 Something dark you wear over your eyes to protect them from bright light. _____

3 You need one to tell the time. You usually wear it on your arm. _____

4 It's sweet and very cold. It sometimes comes in a cone. _____

5 You can listen to music with these, but no one else can hear it. _____

6 Birds can make their nests in it. You can sit in its shade. _____

2 Match the words in 1 to the pictures.

a ▢ b ▢ c ▢
d ▢ e ▢ f ▢

3 Solve the code and write the message.

CODE CRACKER

Mfu't hp   po   b   tdbwfohfs   ivou.

Let's _____ _____ ___ _____ _____ .

Clues

VOCABULARY

I will learn words for possessions.

1 Look and write.

_____ _____ _____ _____

2 Answer the riddles.

1 I have numbers on my face. You wear me. What am I?   _____

2 People use me to keep their pants up. What am I?   _____

3 People make me with their fingers on surfaces. What am I?   _____

4 We are worn as decoration on ears. What are we?   _____

5 I take other people's things and sometimes go to jail. What am I?   _____

6 I am round, and people wear me on their fingers. What am I?   _____

3 Write a riddle with a partner. Share your riddle with the class.

_____

4 Ph Read the sentences. Circle the correct ending sounds of the underlined words. Listen, check, and say.

1	A thief <u>walked</u> into the museum.	/t/	/d/
2	He <u>looked</u> at the ring on display.	/t/	/d/
3	He <u>opened</u> the case.	/t/	/d/
4	He <u>reached</u> for the ring.	/t/	/d/
5	But the museum guard <u>rushed</u> into the room.	/t/	/d/
6	He <u>knocked</u> down the thief.	/t/	/d/
7	She <u>called</u> the police.	/t/	/d/
8	They <u>followed</u> the thief.	/t/	/d/

 use words for possessions.

Language lab

GRAMMAR: SHORT/LONG EVENTS IN THE PAST

I will talk about two events happening in the past.

1 Complete the story with the correct form of the words in brackets.

I was playing in the park when I **1** _____ (hear) a dog bark. When I looked around, a man **2** _____ (put) a rope around the dog's neck. He **3** _____ (pull) the dog along the path when a woman shouted "Stop! That's my dog!" She **4** _____ (trip) and fell when she was running after the man. I **5** _____ (run) after the thief when the dog escaped. It ran back to its owner.

2 Read the story and complete the questions.

The children were changing their clothes after swimming class when Celia screamed. Everyone stopped and looked around. "Who stole my new sneakers?" shouted Celia. She was crying. The teacher was just coming into the changing room. She saw Celia crying and heard what she said. "OK, everyone. Stop what you're doing and look for Celia's shoes." Everyone started to look for the sneakers. The teacher was watching everybody when Trisha found the sneakers under a bench. Celia looked embarrassed. All the other girls were feeling angry.

"You see, Celia?" said the teacher. "No one stole your shoes. You didn't put them away! Apologize right now."

"I'm sorry," said Celia.

came   doing   found   were
what   when   when   told

1   What _____ the children doing _____ Celia screamed?

2   _____ was Celia doing when the teacher _____ into the changing room?

3   What was the teacher _____ when Trisha _____ the sneakers?

4   How were the other girls feeling _____ the teacher _____ Celia to apologize?

3 Work in pairs. Ask and answer the questions in 2.

4 What were the children doing when the recess bell rang? Look and write.

Amy / feed / rabbits

Amy was feeding the rabbits
when the recess bell rang.

Jack / climb / tree

_____
_____

Dan and Henry / play / soccer

_____
_____

They / jump / rope

_____
_____

Suzie / eat / pizza

_____
_____

Ellie / read / book

_____
_____

5 Look at the pictures in 4 again. Listen to the questions and circle the correct answers.

1 Yes, she was. / No, she wasn't.   2 Yes, he was. / No, he wasn't.

3 Yes, they were. / No, they weren't.   4 Yes, they were. / No, they weren't.

5 Yes, they were. / No, they weren't.   6 Yes, she was. / No, she wasn't.

6 Write questions about yesterday.

1 What / teacher / do / you / arrive / class
   What _____ ?

2 What / you / do / friend / arrive / school
   What _____ ?

3 What / you / do / bell / ring / for class
   What _____ ?

I can   talk about two events happening in the past.

81

Story lab

READING

I will read a story about a secret message.

A secret message

1 Read *A Secret Message* again. **Number the events in the correct order.**

a   Harriet was writing out the sentences when the others went to the Viking museum. ☐

b   She didn't hear the question so she couldn't answer it. ☐

c   Harriet was dreaming when Miss Brown asked her a question. ☐ 1

d   She told her to write "I must listen to my teacher" one hundred times. ☐

e   Harriet discovered a secret message on the paper. ☐

f   The security guard and Harriet found that the belt was missing. ☐

g   A thief was going to steal a gold belt from the museum! ☐

h   Miss Brown was wearing the gold belt! ☐

i   Harriet ran to the museum fast. ☐

j   They followed a piece of green wool to Miss Brown. ☐

2 Answer the questions about the story.

1   What did Harriet find when she was writing the sentences for Miss Brown?

_____

2   What was missing in the exhibition?

_____

3   How did the security guard and Harriet know that Miss Brown was the thief?

_____

3 Read and solve the math problems.

MATH ZONE

Harriet had to write 100 lines but she only wrote three quarters of her lines. How many lines did she write?

The museum was 1 mile from the school and Harriet ran at 6 miles per hour. How long did it take her to get to the museum?

4 Find words or phrases in *A Secret Message* that mean:

1   a school outing   _____

2   not having a smooth surface   _____

3   hidden information in writing   _____

4   perhaps   _____

5   figure out the clues   _____

6   jewelry you wear on your wrist   _____

5 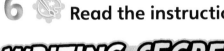 Work in pairs. Discuss the questions.

1   Can you describe Harriet's behavior in beginning of the story?

2   What was Miss Brown's behavior like?

3   Was Harriet's punishment fair or unfair?

4   Was she right to go to the museum alone?

6 Read the instructions. Make invisible ink.

WRITING SECRET MESSAGES IS FUN!

Pretend to be a secret agent and write a secret message to other secret agents! You can write it in invisible ink.

| Squeeze half a lemon into a cup. | Add a few drops of water, and mix. | Write your message with a cotton bud on white paper. |

Let your secret message dry. How can another secret agent read your message?
The secret agent holds the message close to a lamp and waits. Look! The message appears!

7 Where's the thief? Write a message to another secret agent using invisible ink. Can the other agent read your message? Write the message you received.

_____

 I can read a story about a secret message.

Experiment lab

I will find out about the history of codes and ciphers.

1 💡 **Read *Codes and Ciphers* on page 96 of your Student's Book again. Then match to make sentences.**

1	Mary Queen of Scots	**a**	used binary code.
2	Julius Caesar used D	**b**	wrote secret messages in prison.
3	There are only two written symbols	**c**	in secret codes.
4	The first emails	**d**	instead of A in his cipher.
5	People encrypt information	**e**	in a binary code.

2 **Read the text below and circle T (True) or F (False).**

1	George Washington spied against the British.	T / F
2	His secret agent name was 007.	T / F
3	He needed to communicate with his soldiers.	T / F
4	He wrote messages to his soldiers in code.	T / F
5	Washington invented invisible ink on his own.	T / F
6	The British won the War of Independence.	T / F

One of the most famous spies in American history was George Washington. He was a political leader and a military general. When he was a secret agent, his secret agent name was 711. He was head of a very successful group of spies who collected information on the movement of enemy soldiers. He led the American forces in their War of Independence against the British. He later became the first President of the United States. During the revolution, he had to send messages to his soldiers. He didn't want the enemy to read and understand the messages, so he wrote them in cipher. His secret messages helped the United States defeat the British army. To keep the messages extra secret, Washington helped a man called James Jay to create an invisible ink. This was the first invisible ink in history.

3 Answer the questions.

1 What did Washington's spy group do?

_____

2 Why did Washington write messages in code?

_____

3 Who did he write them to?

_____

4 What was Washington called when he was a secret agent?

_____

5 What did Washington help James Jay do?

_____

EXPERIMENT TIME

Report

1 Write the steps you took to create your cipher.

_____

_____

_____

_____

2 Write a report about your experiment. Did the experiment work? Why? Why not?

My experiment worked/didn't work because _____ .

One thing that worked well was _____ .

One thing that didn't work well was _____ .

I learned to _____ .

I enjoyed/didn't enjoy it because _____ _____ .

I know about the history of codes and ciphers.

Are you sure?

COMMUNICATION: HOW CERTAIN YOU ARE

I will express how certain I am.

1 Work in pairs. Read the clues and talk about who you think has Jonathan's skateboard now. How certain are you? Who stole Jonathan's skateboard?

Jonathan is in the park. His skateboard has disappeared. There were only four other people in the park at the time …

Davey is a friend of Jonathan's. He loves skateboarding, but he doesn't have a skateboard. He lost his board a month ago.

Samantha was playing in the park for 15 minutes and then went home. Nobody knows Samantha.

Peter is only 6. He's very good at roller-skating. He wants to have a skateboard, but his mom thinks they're dangerous.

All the children know the ice cream lady. She's very popular in the park. She has a son of her own. He'll be 11 next week.

I think … What about you?

It could be … because …

Are you sure?

It might be …

It must be …

Yes, I'm certain.

2 Write your conclusions. Share them with the class.

I can express how certain I am.

Writing lab

WRITING A DIARY

I will write a diary entry.

1 Share a code you have created with a partner. Then write your partner's code.

2 Write about a time you lost something, or something was stolen from you.

> One day I was walking home from school when I dropped some money. I didn't notice ...

3 Use the secret code you learned in 1 to write one more line about how you felt in 2.

★ ✳ ✧ ✦   ✧   ☆ ★ → ⇛ → ⇨ ➤   ✧

➡ ➤ ★ ✧ →   ✧   → ⇛ ★ ★ ✱ ⇥ ⇢

➤ ✶ ➡ ✳

4 Swap diaries with your partner. Can you decode your partner's code in 3?

_____

_____

_____

_____

I can write a diary entry.

PROJECT AND REVIEW UNIT 6

Create a scavenger hunt

1 Review the scavenger hunt. Complete the chart.

Which hidden items did you find?	Which codes were difficult to crack?
We found _____ _____ _____ _____ _____ _____ _____	The first code was _____ . There was a _____ .
	Which codes were easy to crack?
	It was easy to crack _____ . The easiest _____ .
	Write an example of a code you read.
	_____ _____

2 Complete your project report.

OUR SCAVENGER HUNT

3 Present your report to your family and friends.

I can create a scavenger hunt.

1 Read and sort.

belt earrings find follow clues lose necklace police
ring search thief sneakers sunglasses wristwatch

clothes and accessories	people	actions

2 Read and circle the correct words.

1 I (ate) / was eating my breakfast when they (stole) / were stealing my ring.

2 I (ate) / was eating a snack when they (found) / were finding my backpack.

3 What were you doing before you (were falling) / fell over?

4 I (was playing) / played volleyball when I (was losing) / lost my ring.

5 What was she doing when her shoe (was breaking) / broke .

6 She (wasn't running) / didn't run when her shoe (was breaking) / broke .

7 What were they doing when they (were seeing) / saw the bird ?

8 They (were looking) / looked at the clouds when they (were seeing) / saw the bird.

9 What was he doing when the man (was running) / ran in front of him?

10 He (was following) / followed a clue when the man (was running) / ran in front of him.

3 Read the secret message and write.

A	B	C	D	E	F	G	H	I	J	K	L	M	N	O	P	Q	R	S	T	U	V	W	X	Y	Z
z	y	x	w	v	u	t	s	r	q	p	o	n	m	l	k	j	i	h	g	f	e	d	c	b	a

BLF ZIV Z TIVZG WVGVXGREV

4 Write a secret message for your partner using the code in 3.

_____

_____

Now go to your Progress Chart on page 4.

89

3 Checkpoint

1  Listen and follow Alina's path.

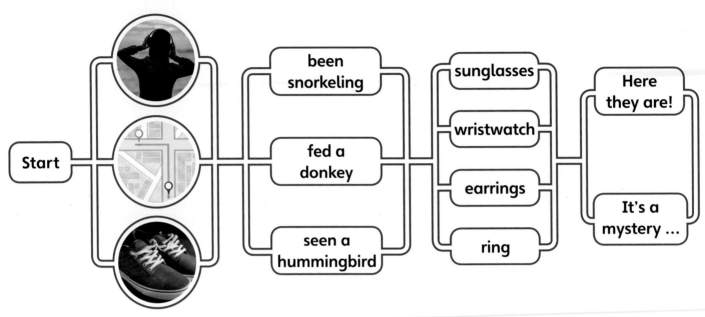

```
Start
    been snorkeling      sunglasses      Here they are!
    fed a donkey         wristwatch
                         earrings        It's a mystery …
    seen a hummingbird   ring
```

2 Listen again and check ☑ the things Alina has done.

1	been snorkeling	2	fed a donkey
3	seen a hummingbird	4	been to a desert island
5	been camping	6	been hiking
7	been ziplining	8	swum in the ocean
9	climbed up a tower	10	walked on the beach
11	visited a palace	12	flown in a helicopter

3 ⚙ Write a paragraph about something you have done. Share details of your experience.

I have …

4 Read the article and circle T (True) or F (False).

Mystery thieves of Christmas Island

January 4th

coconut crab

Christmas Island is a remote and beautiful island off the north coast of Australia. There are beaches for swimming and snorkeling, rainforests for hiking, and spectacular waterfalls where tourists enjoy taking photographs.

However, the island was also home to a curious crime not long ago. Dr. Helen Barnwell, a research scientist from London, visited the island to study a group of local marsupials called sugar gliders. One evening, she set up a special camera in the trees to photograph these interesting animals. But the next morning when she went to check her camera, it wasn't there. She looked around and saw some marks on the ground.

sugar glider

Local police officer Gloria Hann solved the mystery for Dr. Barnwell. Officer Hann said, "The local coconut crabs are the thieves. They have lived on the island for hundreds of years. They grab things they think are food and carry them away to their holes. We call them robber crabs!"

camera

1	Christmas island is located off the south coast of Australia.	T / F
2	Dr. Barnwell lives on Christmas island.	T / F
3	She set her camera up in the morning.	T / F
4	Coconut crabs have lived on the island for many years	T / F
5	They are called robber crabs because they take things.	T / F

5 Put the words in order and write questions. Then, ask a partner.

1   Have / a tablet / you / broken / ? / ever

_____

2   you / Have / ? / any / money / ever / found

_____

3   ever / ? / Have / you / lost / sunglasses / a pair of

_____

The Romans

1 Are these sports and games popular in your country? Have you ever seen or played any of them? Ask and answer.

hula hoop

car racing

chess

Hula hooping is popular in my country.

I've seen car racing.

I've played chess.

2 Read and number the pictures in order.

Ancient Romans loved sports. There were indoor and outdoor sports. A popular sport was hoop rolling. Ancient Roman children rolled their hoops by hitting them with a stick. They had races to see who could roll their hoop fastest.

Chariot racing was very popular, too. The chariots were pulled by horses. The charioteers drove their chariots 8.4 kilometers around an oval arena. They drove them very fast. The winner won a crown of leaves and a lot of money.

Ludus latrunculorum was an inside sport. It was a board game. Players practiced military tactics. It was very popular because the Ancient Romans were great soldiers.

3 Which modern sports in **1** are like the Ancient Roman sports?

Chariot racing: _____   Hoop rolling: _____

Ludus latrunculorum: _____

4  Listen and complete.

> each other   Gladiator events   The rich   stars today   most popular

Glorious Gladiators

Ancient Romans loved going to the amphitheater to watch different events. **1** _____ _____ were one of the **2** _____ _____ sports in Ancient Rome, as well as chariot racing. Two gladiators fought **3** _____ _____ . They wore helmets and carried shields. Gladiators were very brave. **4** _____ _____ and the poor were gladiator fans. Everyone went to watch the events. Successful gladiators were loved and admired by Ancient Romans. They were like soccer, basketball, and baseball **5** _____ _____ !

5 Read and circle the correct answers.

1   Gladiator events / Horse racing were the most popular sports in Ancient Rome.
2   Two / Three gladiators took part in the competition.
3   They were very brave / shy .
4   They had helmets and shields / boots and shields for protection.
5   No one / Everyone watched gladiator events.
6   They admired / were angry with the gladiators.

6 Imagine you are a Roman sportsperson. Write about your day.

I am a charioteer. Today I raced around the Colosseum. I won the race. Then I ...

I know about different festivals.

What shall we eat?

How can we invent a lunch menu?

1 🎧 037 Complete the conversation. Then listen and check.

> haven't   frozen   yogurt   mango   pineapple   would   sweet

Milkshakes
• chocolate • strawberry •
• vanilla •

Frozen yogurt
• Honey and nuts •
• Mango and pineapple •
• Kiwi and candy •

Beatriz: What **1** _____ you like, Jimmy?
A milkshake or a frozen yogurt?

Jimmy: I'd like a **2** _____ _____ , please.

Beatriz: What kind?

Jimmy: **3** _____ and **4** _____ , please.
I like fruit flavors.

Beatriz: Have you ever tried kiwi and candy?

Jimmy: No, I **5** _____ . It sounds **6** _____ .

2 Solve the code. What is Cody asking for?

CODE CRACKER

A   E   O   L   M   P   R   S

_____   _____ !

3 Play *Memory* in groups.

I went to the store and I bought ... honey!

I went to the store and I bought honey and ... apples!

I went to the store and I bought honey, apples, and ...

At the market

VOCABULARY

I will learn words for food and cooking.

1 **Look and write. Which things do you like cooking with?**

1 s_____

2 s_____

3 v_____

4 h_____

5 f_____

6 o_____

2 **Work in pairs. Look at the pictures in 1 for one minute. Then cover the pictures and test each other's memories.**

What's number 4?

Umm … I think it's herbs.

Yes, that's right.

3 **Unscramble the words and complete the recipe for crepes.**

LFURO   HNEOY   BUETTR   NTSU   GEG

HONEY AND NUT CREPES

⬡ Mix one cup of **1** _____ , one tablespoon of oil, two cups of milk, and one **2** _____ in a bowl.

⬡ Heat a pan. Add a tablespoon of **3** _____ .

⬡ Pour some of the crepe mixture into the hot pan and cook until bubbles form.

⬡ Turn it over and cook it on the other side for 1 minute.

⬡ Pour **4** _____ and sprinkle **5** _____ on top of the crepe, fold and serve.

I can use words for food and cooking.

Language lab

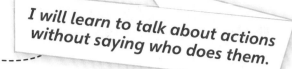

I will learn to talk about actions without saying who does them.

1 **Complete the sentences with the correct form of the words in brackets.**

1   Honey _____ (use) sometimes instead of sugar.

2   Yogurt _____ (make) from milk.

3   Green tea _____ (drink) in China.

4   Peanuts _____ (grow) underground.

5   A lot of sushi _____ (eat) in Japan.

2 **Write questions. Remember to use the past participle.**

1   What / popcorn / make / from?

   _____?

2   How / milkshakes / make?

   _____?

3   Where / rice / grow?

   _____?

4   Where / salt / find?

   _____?

3 **Read and number the pictures in the correct order.**

From cocoa to chocolate

Chocolate is made from cocoa beans. Cocoa beans are found in pods on cacao trees.

The pods are opened. There are about 50 beans in each pod.

The beans are dried in the sun and they are sent to chocolate manufacturers all over the world.

The beans are crushed and mixed with milk and sugar.

Finally, the chocolate is heated and poured into molds.

The finished chocolates are sent to stores and are sold. Then they are eaten by hungry people like you and me. Delicious!

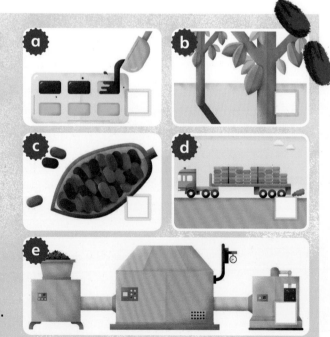

4 Look at 3. Underline all the examples of present passive verbs.

5 🎧 038 Complete the information about cotton candy. Then listen and check.

> Cotton candy is very popular. It **1** _____ (make) from sugar, water, corn syrup, and a little salt. Food coloring **2** _____ (use) to color the candy blue, green, pink, or yellow. The ingredients **3** _____ (heat), then spun around a stick. It is sold on street corners.

6 💡 Read and number the steps in the correct order.

How
Mexican Hot Chocolate is made.

a First, milk is measured and warmed. ☐

b The milk and chocolate mixture are boiled and cinnamon is added. ☐

c Then chocolate is broken up and put into the warm milk. ☐

d Then the hot chocolate is poured into mugs. Marshmallows are not added to Mexican hot chocolate. ☐

e After the spice has been added, the mixture is stirred with a special whisk to add air. ☐

7 🗨 Test your partner by asking them questions about cotton candy and hot chocolate.

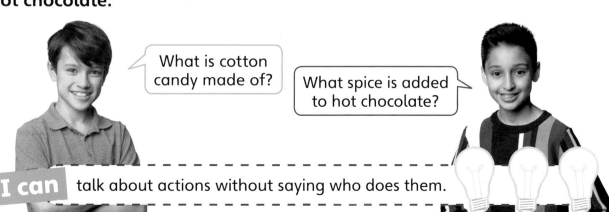

What is cotton candy made of?

What spice is added to hot chocolate?

I can talk about actions without saying who does them.

Story lab

I will read a story about making soup.

TASTY SOUP

1 **Read *Tasty Soup* again. Then answer the questions.**

1 What was Antonio's problem?

Antonio was _____ .

2 Did the villagers want to help him at first?

_____

3 What did Antonio do when he reached the stream?

He _____ .

4 Who was the first person to help him?

The first person to help him was _____ .

5 How did the villagers help him in the end?

They _____ .

6 What did the villagers add to the meal at the end?

They _____ .

2 **Correct the false sentences.**

1 Rosa was the first person to help Antonio.

_____

2 Antonio wanted to make salad in his cooking pot.

_____

3 The stone in the story was really magic.

_____

4 The villagers brought fruit to Antonio.

_____

5 They all ate the magic stone.

_____

6 The final meal smelled disgusting.

_____

3 ☼ Match the words to their meaning.

1 cooking pot
2 stone
3 soup
4 herbs
5 beans
6 meat

a a liquid meal eaten with a spoon
b animal which is eaten as food
c hot food is made in it
d a small piece of rock
e added to food to make it tasty
f pulses you can eat

4 Complete the sentences.

1 Antonio was looking for food because he was very _____ .

2 He tricked the villagers by telling them that the stone was _____ .

3 Antonio told one of the village women that the soup was a bit too _____ .

4 The soup smelled very good, but it wasn't _____ enough. Thanks to Rosa the problem was solved!

5 In the end the soup was delicious. Everyone said it was very _____ .

5 ☐ In groups, share your ideas about these questions. Give reasons for your answers.

Why do you think Antonio was so hungry?

Why do you think Antonio added a stone to his pot of boiling water?

What was Rosa like at the beginning of the story?

Was Antonio a good man or an untrustworthy man?

6 Read and solve the math problems.

MATH ZONE

If four villagers each add 3 ingredients to the soup, how many ingredients are added? _____

If each extra ingredient weighs 25g, how much weight is added to the soup? _____

I can read a story about making soup.

Experiment lab

I will find out about solutions and mixtures.

1 Complete the sentences.

1   Sea water consists of _____ and water.

2   Salt is a _____ substance.

3   Sand is an _____ substance.

4   Sand and water mix but don't make a _____ .

5   Too much sugar or salt in foods is _____ .

| bad for you |
| insoluble |
| salt |
| soluble |
| solution |

2 Answer the questions.

1   Why are soda drinks often unhealthy?

_____

2   What happens when water is boiled?

_____

3   What happens when sea water is boiled?

_____

4   How can a mixture of water and sand be separated?

_____

5   For a healthy diet, what advice should be followed?

_____

3 Match the sentences to the pictures.

1   He's heating the mixture.

2   The water is bubbling in a pot.

3   He's putting a spoonful of salt into water.

4   He's mixing it and the salt is dissolving.

5   The water has evaporated and there is salt at the bottom of the pot.

4 Work in pairs. Read these nutritional labels. Which is the healthier snack? Why?

Nutrition Facts

Serving Size   About 12 chips (28g)

Amount per serving

Calories 150

	% Daily Value*
Total Fat 8g	**10%**
Saturated Fat 1g	6%
Trans Fat 0g	
Cholesterol 0mg	**0%**

BONGOS
TORTILLA CHIPS
NACHO CHEESE

GOLDEN BIRD
Almonds
SNACK CRACKERS
CHEDDAR CHEESE
Made with real almonds!
Gluten Free

Nutrition Facts

Serving Size   1 bag (57g)

Amount per serving

Calories 250

	% Daily Value*
Total Fat 7g	**9%**
Saturated Fat 1g	5%
Trans Fat 0g	
Cholesterol 0mg	**0%**

EXPERIMENT TIME

Report

1 Write your report.

1 I washed and dried a glass. I checked that it was clean and completely dry.
2 I filled the glass with warm water.
3 I put a teaspoon of oil into the glass of warm water.
4 I took a spoon and mixed the oil and water.
5 I mixed it for 30 seconds. The oil did not dissolve.
6 I mixed it for 30 more seconds. The oil still did not dissolve.
7 My conclusion is that oil is insoluble.

2 Continue your experiment. Use these substances. Record your results.

chalk

dish detergent

I know about solutions and mixtures.

Ordering food

COMMICATION: *TOO MUCH / NOT ENOUGH*

I will talk about quantities and order food.

1 Paul and his sister Nancy are shopping to buy food for a picnic. Listen and circle T (True) or F (False).

1 Nancy is very happy with the contents of the shopping cart.   T / F
2 Nancy says there's too much salt in potato chips.   T / F
3 Nancy asks Paul to put three apples in the cart.   T / F
4 Nancy wants to make cheese sandwiches for the picnic.   T / F
5 They're meeting their friends in the garden.   T / F

2 Look at the pictures. Talk about what Paul and Nancy said about the picnic.

> There are too many sandwiches.

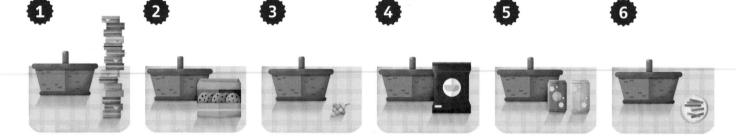

3 In groups of three, role-play the conversation between the children who have arrived at the picnic and their friend Erin.

Nancy: Would you like a sandwich?

Erin: Yes, please.

Paul: Would you prefer a cheese and tomato sandwich or a chicken and lettuce sandwich?

Erin: Chicken and lettuce sounds delicious. I'll have one of those.

Paul: Here you are.

Erin: Do you have mayonnaise?

Nancy: Yes, here you are.

Erin: Thank you.

4 In groups of three, role-play a new conversation for you.

> Would you like …?   Would you prefer …?   Do you have …?

I can talk about quantities and order food.

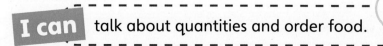

Writing lab

WRITING A RECIPE

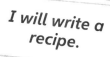

I will write a recipe.

1 🎧 040 **Listen to the recipe and check ☑ the ingredients you need.**

☐ apples ☐ honey ☐ flour ☐ pepper ☐ milk
☐ bananas ☐ eggs ☐ butter ☐ coconut
☐ sugar ☐ cream ☐ salt ☐ nuts

2 Listen again and complete the recipe card.

Banana muffins

Ingredients

3 large bananas

_____

_____

_____

_____

3 Complete the instructions for making banana muffins.

> Add   Bake   Pour   Mix   Heat

1 _____ together the sugar, flour, and salt.

2 _____ the butter in the microwave until it melts.

3 _____ the butter, egg, and milk to the muffin mixture and mix.

4 _____ the mixture into a muffin pan.

5 _____ the muffins for twenty minutes at 180°C.

4 Read the beginning of the story, then write the ending.

It was Mitch's birthday. Six of his best friends were invited for a picnic in the yard. Mitch wanted to make mango muffins for the party. Mango muffins are made with mangoes, but Mitch didn't have enough mangoes in the house. There wasn't enough butter either. So, Mitch took some money out of his piggy bank and

_____

_____

I can write a recipe.

PROJECT AND REVIEW UNIT 7

Invent a lunch menu

Project report

1 Complete the chart.

What dishes did you include on your menu?		What did your menu look like? It had ...	
☐ chicken	☐ fruit	☐ starters	☐ main courses
☐ vegetables	☐ ice cream	☐ desserts	☐ descriptions of food
☐ chocolate	☐ pizza	☐ ingredients	☐ clear writing
☐ nuts	☐ other	☐ decoration	
Did you role-play using your menu with another group?		**Did you role-play using another group's menu?**	
☐ They chose things from our menu.		☐ We chose things from their menu.	
☐ They wrote a review.		☐ We wrote a review.	
☐ We read reviews of our menu.		☐ They read our reviews.	
What did other groups say about your menu?			
They liked _____			
and _____ . They said _____ .			

2 Complete your project report. Use your dictionary to help you.

Report – Invent a lunch menu

First, we _____ .

Our menu _____ .

We role-played _____ .

They said our menu was _____ .

3 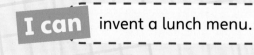 Share your report about the project with another group.

I can invent a lunch menu.

1 Read and sort.

meat   spices   mango   strawberries   vegetables
herbs   flour   oil   nuts   sugar   salt   honey   pineapple

pizza	ice cream

2 Write questions. Remember to use the past participle.

1   Where / rice / grow
    Where is rice grown?

2   What / ice cream / make of
    _____

3   What / spices / use for
    _____

4   How / donuts / cook
    _____

5   How long / pasta / cook for
    _____

6   What / cheese / make from
    _____

3 Complete the sentences with the correct form of the words in brackets.

1   Rice _____ (grow) in China.
2   Ice cream _____ (make) of cream, milk, and sugar.
3   Spices _____ (use) for flavor.
4   Donuts _____ (drop) into hot oil.
5   Fresh pasta _____ (cook) for 2–3 minutes.

4 Jay and Liz are having a party, but Liz is worried. Circle the correct answers.

1   Do we have enough / too many food?
2   I think we've got too many / too much nuts.
3   We have too many / too much ice cream.
4   We don't have enough / too many pizzas.
5   Are there enough / too much bananas?

>>> **Now go to your Progress Chart on page 4.**

8 Our digital world!

How can we create a song about technology?

1 Read and sort.

> email   headphones   famous   prize   trumpet   song   website   guitar
> winner   cell phone   screen   keyboard   speaker   microphone

digital device	musical	contest

2 Unscramble the words to complete the sentences. Listen and check.

> ETWIEBS
> ORADYKEB
> PCOMREOIHN
> IGRTUA
> GONS
> HOSDHAENPE
> CLLE PHNEO
> KSEREPA

CODE CRACKER

First, look up a songwriting **1** _____ online to learn how to write a song. Second, write lyrics for your **2** _____ . Next, get your **3** _____ or **4** _____ out and create music to go with your lyrics. Then connect your **5** _____ to your **6** _____ or **7** _____ and sing! Use your **8** _____ _____ to make a video of yourself singing your song. Play it back and watch yourself.

3 Add these words to the chart in 1.

> text message   compete   notes   songbook   video game control

How do we use technology?

I will learn words to talk about technology.

VOCABULARY

1 **Complete the crossword.**

Across

3 a page on the internet where you can find information about something

8 a device that you wear over your ears to listen to the radio or music

9 the part of a television or computer where you can see images or information

Down

1 a musical instrument with six strings that you play with your fingers

2 something you can call your friends on

4 a short piece of music with words that you sing

5 a word meaning "known by many people"

6 an electronic musical instrument that is like a piano

7 something you can win in a competition or a race

2 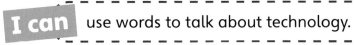 **Complete the chant. Listen and check. Then recite the chant.**

> download   listen   look up   record   use

I use my devices every day.
I use my computer in many ways.
Press a button. Check a site.
Send an email. What to write?
I use my devices every day.
I **1** _____ my tablet in many ways.
2 _____ to music. **3** _____ apps.
4 _____ a message. **5** _____ maps.

3  **Write a new verse about cell phones.**

I use my devices every day.
I use my cell phone in many ways.

I can use words to talk about technology.

Language lab

GRAMMAR: TAG QUESTIONS

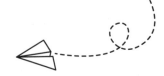

I will check information using tag questions.

1 **Read and circle the correct tags.**

1 This computer game is great, is it? / isn't it? / isn't she?

2 We can't use this tablet to take photos, can we? / can't we? / can they?

3 You like playing the violin, do they? / do you? / don't you?

4 These magazines aren't very interesting, aren't they? / are they? / isn't it?

5 I'm not early, am I? / can I? / aren't I?

2 **Complete the sentences with the correct tags. Then listen and check.**

1 Mary can ride a horse, _____ .

2 The bus comes at 7:00, _____ .

3 Your sister isn't in our class, _____ .

4 Tomorrow is your birthday, _____ .

5 They taste like peaches, _____ .

3 **Do the general knowledge quiz. Circle the correct answers.**

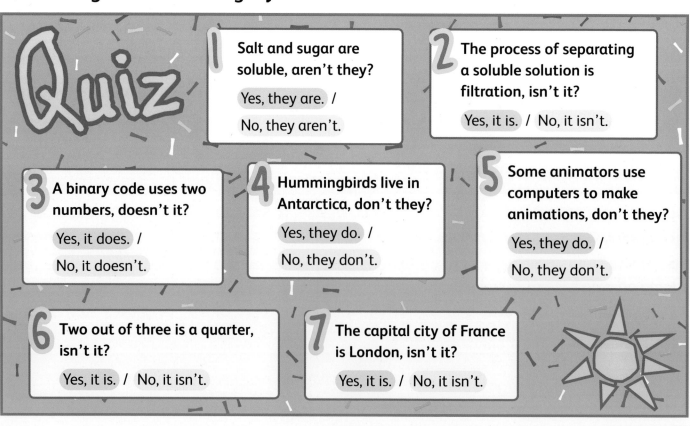

Quiz

1 Salt and sugar are soluble, aren't they?

Yes, they are. / No, they aren't.

2 The process of separating a soluble solution is filtration, isn't it?

Yes, it is. / No, it isn't.

3 A binary code uses two numbers, doesn't it?

Yes, it does. / No, it doesn't.

4 Hummingbirds live in Antarctica, don't they?

Yes, they do. / No, they don't.

5 Some animators use computers to make animations, don't they?

Yes, they do. / No, they don't.

6 Two out of three is a quarter, isn't it?

Yes, it is. / No, it isn't.

7 The capital city of France is London, isn't it?

Yes, it is. / No, it isn't.

4 Put the words in order and make sentences with tag questions. Match and write them under the pictures. Then say the answers.

a strong / they / aren't / are / they

b don't / they / look / delicious / they

c red / she / has / doesn't / hair / she

d play / loves / he / soccer / doesn't / to / he

 **1**

 **2**

 **3**

 **4**

_____ _____ _____ _____

_____ _____ _____ _____

_____ _____ _____ _____

5 Complete the questions. Then ask and answer with a partner.

1 You _____ in the 5th grade, aren't you?

2 You like chocolate, _____ ?

3 You _____ sick today, are you?

4 You _____ play volleyball, do you?

6 Look at the picture and make some guesses about the person. Use tag questions.

Age: She's _____ years old, isn't she?

Nationality: She's _____ , isn't she?

Sport: She loves _____ , _____ ?

Favorite gadget: It's her _____ _____ ?

Favorite place: It's the _____ _____ ?

7 044 Now listen and check your guesses in 6.

 I can check information using tag questions.

Story lab

READING

I will read a story about a competition.

THE COMPETITION

1  **Read *The Competition* again. Number the events in the correct order.**

a   Lily and Tyler noticed a poster about a walking competition. ☐

b   Tyler and Lily checked the big screen in the town square. ☐

c   Lily was disappointed she was losing so she went home. ☐

d   The screen showed that Lily didn't have as many points as Tyler. ☐

e   They downloaded an app to count their steps. ☐

f   During the competition they walked thousands of steps every day. ☐

g   Tyler went to Lily's house and discovered that she was cheating. ☐

2 Read and circle T (True) or F (False).

1   The app is downloaded onto a cell phone.   T / F

2   The app records time.   T / F

3   The app sends information to be displayed on a big screen.   T / F

4   The person who has walked the least steps is the winner.   T / F

5   Tyler wasn't good at many things.   T / F

6   Lily was good at many things.   T / F

3 Check ☑ the conversation you think matches the picture. Discuss why with a partner.

a ☐   "You like walking, don't you?" asked Lily.
"Yes, I do," answered Tyler. "Let's enter. It won't be easy, but I think it will be fun!"

b ☐   "Look!" shouted a little boy, 10 minutes later.
"Lily's score is going up really fast."
"Look! She's done 57,300 steps … no, 57,400 …"
"You're kidding."

c ☐   "Oh, Lily," he said. "The app thought you were walking."
"Sorry," said Lily. "I was cheating. I wanted to win. It was silly."

4 Punctuate the conversation. Use quotation marks (" "), commas (,), question marks (?), and periods (.)

You like engineering don't you Tyler asked Lily

Yes I do answered Lily

There's a competition downtown next week said Tyler

Let's enter it! exclaimed Lily excitedly

5 Read and solve the math problems.

MATH ZONE

Abby entered the same walking competition as Tyler and Lily. The first day she walked 6,920 steps, the second day she walked 7,000 steps, and the third day she walked 4,080 steps.

1   How many steps did Abby walk altogether?

_____

2   What was the average number of steps she walked a day? _____

3   How many more steps will she need to reach 20,000? _____

6 Circle the correct tags. Then ask and answer about the story with a partner.

1   Lily is embarrassed, is she / isn't she ? Why?

2   It isn't good to cheat, is it / isn't it ? Why?

3   Tyler is a good friend, is he / isn't he ? Why?

I can read a story about a competition.

Experiment lab

I will find out about electricity.

1 Do the quiz. Circle a or b.

1 Electricity is a type of ...

  a energy.

  b artificial light.

2 The two kinds of energy are ...

  a static and lightning.

  b static and current.

3 Static electricity sometimes forms in ...

  a clouds.

  b circuits.

4 Some appliances use _____ electricity.

  a static

  b current

5 Other appliances use ...

  a batteries.

  b lightning.

6 To power an electrical device, you need a/an ...

  a off switch.

  b circuit.

2 Look at the appliances and check ☑ the ones you have at home.

hair dryer

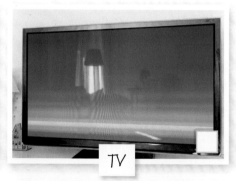

TV

TV remote control

washing machine

remote control helicopter

lamp

3  Work with a partner to guess the form of energy the appliances in 2 use; electrical current (plug in) or batteries (including rechargeable). Then check at home.

> The hairdryer uses an electrical current, doesn't it?

> Yes, it does. The remote control doesn't use electrical current, does it? I think it uses batteries.

4 Choose one of the appliances in 2. How would your life be different without it?

Our washing machine is very useful. We use if often at my house. We need the washing machine to wash our clothes when they are dirty. The washing machine uses electricity to make movement to clean the clothes. Without a washing machine we would have to wash our clothes by hand. I like the washing machine.

EXPERIMENT TIME

Report

1 What did you learn from your experiment?

I learned _____

_____ .

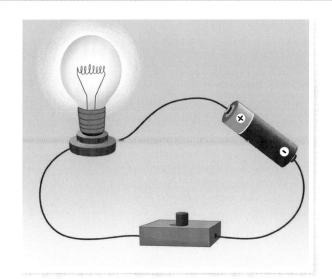

2 Did your experiment work? Write the reasons you think your experiment succeeded or failed.

My experiment worked / failed because

_____

_____ .

I know how an electrical circuit works.

Music and games

COMMUNICATION: –ING OR –ED?

> I will describe things and say how they make me feel.

1 Unscramble the feelings and complete the sentences.

> REDBO EXITEDC FRINEDGHTE INSTTEEDER RELEDAX

1 When I'm about to do something new for the first time, I feel _____ .

2 When I do my deep breathing exercises, I feel _____ .

3 During a very long movie that I'm not interested in, I feel _____ .

4 When someone is teaching me something I want to know, I'm very _____ .

5 When I'm alone in the dark, I feel _____ .

2 Complete. Then listen and check.

1 I'm falling asleep. This movie is so _____ .

2 That Halloween mask is very _____ .

3 The final minutes of a game are often _____ .

4 Listening to the sounds of the ocean is very _____ .

5 Science is much more _____ than math.

3 Read and circle the correct words.

a Dad is interested / interesting in the TV show.

b Alan thinks the show is frightened / frightening .

c Mom thinks the show is excited / exciting .

a The children are bored / boring .

b The show they are watching is very bored / boring .

c They need a more excited / exciting show.

I can describe things and say how they make me feel.

Writing lab

WRITING A STORY FROM PICTURES

I will write a story about some pictures.

1 **Look and write sentences to describe the pictures.**

> children sister brother cousin beach vacation ice cream
> drop lick dog cry sad eat happy relaxed relaxing exciting

1 The dog looks hungry.

2 The children are eating ice cream.

3 _____

4 _____

5 _____

6 _____

7 _____

8 _____

2 **Draw a storyboard for you story.**

One day	Suddenly	Then	In the end

3 **Write the story and add more details.**

_____

_____

_____

_____

4 **Work in pairs. Share your stories.**

I can write a story about some pictures.

PROJECT AND REVIEW UNIT 8

Create a song about technology

1 Complete the chart.

What was your song about?		What sounds did you use in your song?	
☐ tablet	☐ apps	☐ clicking fingers	☐ clapping hands
☐ computer	☐ headphones	☐ stomping	☐ pencils on desks
☐ cell phone	☐ other	☐ scraping chairs	☐ other
What rhythms did you use in your song?		**What symbols did you use for your score?**	
☐ fast and exciting		☐ asterisks	☐ stars
☐ slow and relaxing		☐ wavy lines	☐ other
Did you practice your song?		**What did other groups like about your song?**	
☐ Yes ☐ No		They liked _____ and _____ .	

2 Complete your project report.

What was your song about? _____

What sounds did you use in your song? _____

What rhythms did you use in your song? _____

What symbols did you use for your score? _____

Did you practice your song?   Yes ☐   No ☐

What did other groups like about your song?

They liked _____ and _____ .

3 ⚫ Share your report about the project with another group. Check others' reports using tag questions.

    create a song about technology.

1 Find and circle the words from the unit.

B	P	E	C	E	L	L	P	H	O	N	E	A	T	P
A	P	P	O	C	O	M	K	E	Y	B	O	A	R	D
N	U	T	M	E	R	K	E	A	B	Y	A	O	U	O
D	R	D	P	M	T	R	U	D	M	P	E	T	M	W
G	U	G	U	I	T	A	R	P	G	U	I	I	P	N
S	D	A	T	C	O	L	P	H	U	R	A	I	E	L
C	E	N	E	R	U	P	L	O	A	D	E	R	T	O
R	R	N	R	O	S	P	E	N	K	A	S	P	E	A
C	E	L	L	P	S	C	R	E	E	N	L	P	H	D
O	M	N	E	H	C	F	G	S	P	E	A	K	E	R
C	O	M	P	O	U	T	E	R	A	T	R	U	M	P
K	B	E	Y	N	M	I	C	R	C	E	A	P	P	H
O	N	E	M	E	I	C	K	B	O	A	S	T	A	P

app
band
cell phone
download
computer
guitar
headphones
keyboard
microphone
screen
speaker
trumpet
upload

2 Solve the riddles.

1 I speak into it to make my voice louder. I sing into it with my band. _____

2 I use it to write on my computer. I play music with it. _____

3 I download music onto it. I use it to call my mom. _____

4 I plug them into my cell phone. I can hear well with them. _____

5 It's a musical instrument. It has six strings. I play it in a band. _____

6 It's flat. I can see things on it. My computer, phone, and tablet have one. _____

3 Complete the sentences with tag questions.

1 A singer uses a microphone, _____ _____ ?

2 We can send text messages on our cell phones, _____ _____ ?

3 Some people use websites to help write their songs, _____ _____ ?

4 She isn't famous, _____ _____ ?

5 The contest is tomorrow, _____ _____ ?

Now go to your Progress Chart on page 4.

4 Checkpoint
UNITS 7 AND 8

1 046 **Listen and follow the path.**

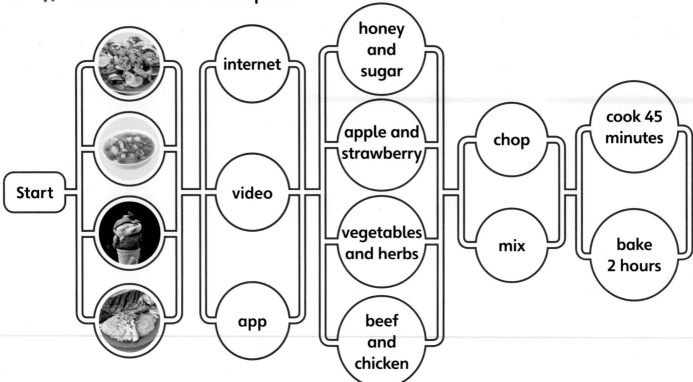

2 **Read the questions and match them with the correct answer.**

a How much butter do we need?   **b** What are we going to make today?
c Where did you find the recipe?   **d** What ingredients do we need?
e How long does it take?

1 _____

Let's make cornbread. I've got a great new recipe!

2 _____

I looked it up on the internet.

3 _____

Fresh corn, butter, salt, milk, and eggs.

4 _____

It says we need about ½ a cup.

5 _____

It says it takes about 10 minutes to prepare and 25 minutes to bake.

3 Read and circle.

1 Avocados are grown in
 a Mexico.   b Antarctica.

2 92% of avocados are grown in
 a Michoacán.   b Oaxaca.

3 Avocados are used to make
 a milkshakes.   b guacamole.

4 340 kilograms are produced every year by
 a one avocado farm.   b one avocado tree.

5 Most avocados are imported by
 a the United States.   b China.

4 Work in pairs. Ask and answer questions about the information in 3.

5 Write everything you have eaten today in the chart. Then discuss it with a partner.

| Write the food and the amount. | Keep a record for the coming week. | Do you have a healthy diet? | How could you change your diet? |

fruit & nuts	vegetables & oils	grains
meat	**sugar**	**dairy**

Celebrating festivals

CULTURE

1 Read and complete the information sheet.

In India, people love festivals. There are a lot of festivals every year. In fact, there are more than 30. And Indian festivals are a lot of fun. For example, there is Holi festival in March. The Holi festival is also called the Festival of Colors. This festival says goodbye to winter and welcomes in the spring. It's a time for people to meet, play, laugh, and forget old fights and arguments.

How do people celebrate the Holi festival? They throw paint powder and colored water all over each other. The paint powder and colored water symbolize happiness and the arrival of brightly colored spring flowers. The Holi festival is a magical time in India.

Name of Festival: _____

Month of Festival: _____

Its popular name: _____

What it celebrates: _____

How it is celebrated: _____

_____

2  In groups, talk about a festival in your country.

When is it?

How do you celebrate?

Are there any special foods/drinks?

Do people wear special clothes or a costume?

3 Write four sentences about a festival you enjoy in your country.

4  **Listen and circle T (True) or F (False).**

1   Jaipur is a city in the south of India.   T / F
2   In India, elephants represent kings and queens for many people.   T / F
3   The Elephant Festival takes place in fall.   T / F
4   At the festival, elephants are decorated with colored flowers.   T / F
5   The best decorated elephant wins a prize.   T / F
6   Elephants take part in sports events at the festival.   T / F

5 **Correct the false statements in 3.**

_____

_____

_____

6 In pairs, decide on a festival to hold where you live. When is it? What does it celebrate? Do people eat special food and wear special clothes? Do they dance, sing, or do special activities? Look at the photos for ideas.

sweet biscuits and other food

special candles

fireworks

7 **Design a poster to advertise the festival you created in 5.**

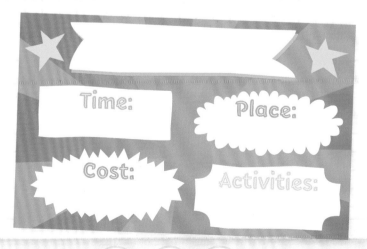
Time: Place:
Cost: Activities:

I know about different festivals.

Extra writing

Unit 1

1 **Write silly instructions using must, must not, have to, and don't have to. Choose from the suggestions or use your own ideas.**

- How to be a bad student.
- How to be a terrible dog owner.
- How to be an annoying neighbor.

> How to be a bad student.
>
> You must arrive late.
>
> You must never do your homework.

Unit 2

1 **Match the poems to the pictures.**

a   A pointy, yellow star, shining brightly in the sky.

b   An exciting small red flower in the desert. It pushes up from the hot ground.

c   A cool, soft and round raindrop. It splashes on the hot pavement. Sizzle! Sizzle!

2 **Choose a word and write it in the center of the word web. Then write as many describing words around it as you can think of.**

pyramid   river   rock   waterfall   lake   raindrop   cloud   snow   desert

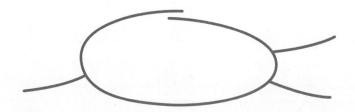

3 **Write a shape poem with your ideas in 2.**

Unit 3

1 Imagine your project festival is happening this weekend. Write notes about what is happening at the festival.

2 Write an email to invite a friend to the festival. Write about the activities, the food, the people, the music, and the shows at the festival.

Hi _____ !

I'm going to the _____ festival this weekend. Do you want to come? This is the plan:

_____

_____

_____

_____

Next, _____

After that, _____

Finally, _____

Say you will come!

From,

Unit 4

1 Complete the profile for your favorite actor.

Name: _____

Nationality: _____

Age: _____

Most famous movies: _____

Characters played: _____

Best performance: _____

2 Write a paragraph about your favorite actor.

_____
_____
_____
_____
_____
_____

Unit 5

1 Read the information about Kenya and check ☑ what you want to do.

Nairobi, Kenya

Full-day tours: ☐ Safari: See rhinos, lions, zebras ☐ Mountain trip: Hike up Mt. Longonot

Half-day tours: ☐ City visit ☐ Zoo: Feed giraffes, elephants

2 Answer the questions a journalist sent you.

Where are you now? _____
_____

What have you done today? _____
_____

Why do you enjoy traveling? _____
_____

Where would you like to go next? _____
_____

3 Swap your answers in 2 with a partner. Write an article about your partner's travels.

Unit 6

1 Write a diary entry about the last time you lost something.

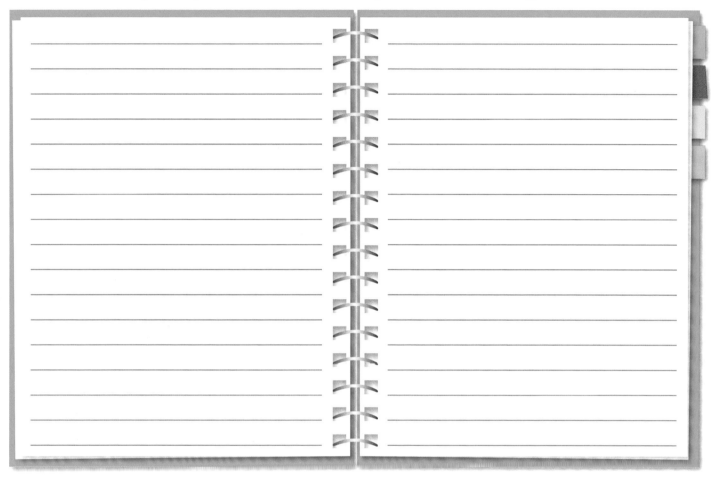

2 Use one of the codes in Unit 6 to write about how you felt.

3 Share your secret message with a partner. Can your partner figure out the message?

1 **Think about a recipe and answer the question.**

What do you want to cook?

_____

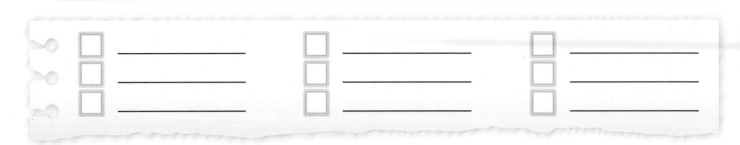

2 **Write a list of ingredients you will need.**

3 **Write instructions for making your dish.**

> add   eat   cook   pour   mix   heat   fill   shape   dip   bake

1 _____
2 _____
3 _____
4 _____
5 _____
6 _____

4 **Draw your dish.**

Unit 8

1 Look at the pictures. Think and write notes about what happened.

Terrible. Listening to music. Using my best friend's tablet, computer, and headphones. Having fun. Feeling excited.

2 Imagine you are telling the story. Write about what happened.

_____

_____

_____

_____

_____

_____

_____

_____

3 Work in pairs. Share your stories.

What happened in your story?

In my story, lots of exciting things happened ...

★ You did it! ★

★ ★ ★ Congratulations! ★ ★ ★

★ Great job! ★

★ Fantastic! ★

★ Super! ★